Praise for
IMMINENT DOMAINS
Reckoning with the Anthropocene

"Naccarato leads us into terrains of complex, contradictory, and intensely entangled curiosity, devastation, rebirth, reckoning, and wonder in these essays—but she does not lead, instead she seeks to take us by the hand—to walk, crawl, writhe, swim, sit, burrow, dissolve into our constituent parts right alongside us. To sing and be heard, to find the song in silence, is this meditation. To hover in making and unmaking amidst the reverberations the material world makes itself into, and what we, as diverse permutations of humans, make of this world. There is great vulnerability here and also the most potent learning for how to reckon with the simultaneous truths of love and damage. Naccarato holds on, and does not let go, even where the pain is deepest."

—Angélique Lalonde, author of *Glorious Frazzled Beings*

"A book so unique it feels like a genre unto itself—an inquest, a love letter, a dirge, an electrifying epic, a timely tincture, a heart-stopping memoir of stones. Alessandra Naccarato takes us across geographical, emotional, and communal domains to the heat points of ecological survival and love. There is gorgeous LIFE in these interlacing essays, which refuse to accept life's brutal and casual devaluation in the name of extractive settler-colonialism. *Imminent Domains* is a beautiful feat of artistry and truth-saying."

—Kyo Maclear, author of *Birds Art Life*

T0035408

"Thoroughly researched and superbly crafted, Alessandra Naccarato's *Imminent Domains* offers us something even more precious than information, or a call-to-arms. It offers recognition, friendship, and the possibility of arriving—across the distance and loneliness introduced by a mounting sense of isolation, loss, and collective despair—a true connection. As a result, it also offers hope. Not as a quick-fix—a way to gloss over or ignore either the (ongoing) violences of the past or the very real challenges that face us now—but instead as an authentic mode of perceiving and activating within personal experience, doubt, and grief, a broader sense of kinship."

—Johanna Skibsrud, author of
The Nothing That Is: Essays on Art, Literature and Being

Praise for
RE-ORIGIN OF SPECIES

Winner of the 2022 AICW Bressani Literary Prize for Poetry
Shortlisted for the 2020 Gerald Lampert Memorial Award
Longlisted for the 2020 Pat Lowther Memorial Award

"Alessandra Naccarato's *Re-Origin of Species* is masterfully crafted. The maturity of these poems is matched by the high-level operation of the themes they enact. Naccarato creates an ecosystem in which self, psyche, and external environment are understood as intrinsically inseparable. Each poem achieves that much sought-after combination of unexpected and inevitable, an indication of high-level functioning both in craft and creative thought. As comfortable in the darkness as in the light, this collection creates an honest beauty and imaginativeness that can't help but strike a chord, or several."

—Gerald Lampert Memorial Award Jury Citation

"*Re-Origin of Species* is a riveting, ambitious book that delivers on its ambition. A litany of sorrows for the world as it is, and a prayer for the future."

—*The British Columbia Review*

"Despite lamenting how humans have imperiled the natural world through our actions, *Re-Origin of Species* does not romanticize nature as an idyllic thing. It is powerful and just as capable of causing pain and death, but it still feels like there is a qualitative difference."

—*Canadian Literature*

Additional Praise for
ALESSANDRA NACCARATO

"Alessandra Naccarato's poems are visually powerful and sensually charged. Her imagery is as unexpected as it is memorable. These are poems adept at evoking the textures and sensations of place, even as they pay careful attention to sound, to the music of the line. Ranging from the sting of personal loss to navigating landscapes full of promise, Naccarato's poetry interrogates the place where the personal meets the wild."

—2015 RBC Bronwen Wallace Jury Citation

IMMINENT DOMAINS

RECKONING

WITH THE

ANTHROPOCENE

ALESSANDRA NACCARATO

IMMINENT DOMAINS

RECKONING WITH THE ANTHROPOCENE

ESSAYS BY
ALESSANDRA NACCARATO

ESSAIS SERIES NO. 14
BOOK*HUG PRESS
TORONTO 2022

Library and Archives Canada Cataloguing in Publication

Title: Imminent domains : reckoning with the Anthropocene /Alessandra Naccarato.
Names: Naccarato, Alessandra, author.
Series: Essais (Toronto, Ont.) ; no. 14.
Description: Series statement: Essais series ; 14 | Essays.
Identifiers: Canadiana (print) 20220217556
Canadiana (ebook) 20220217580
   ISBN 9781771667753 (softcover)
   ISBN 9781771667777 (PDF)
   ISBN 9781771667760 (EPUB)
Subjects: LCGFT: Essays.
Classification: LCC PS8627.A27 I46 2022 | DDC C814/.6—dc23

The production of this book was made possible through the generous assistance of the Canada Council for the Arts and the Ontario Arts Council. Book*hug Press also acknowledges the support of the Government of Canada through the Canada Book Fund and the Government of Ontario through the Ontario Book Publishing Tax Credit and the Ontario Book Fund.

Book*hug Press acknowledges that the land on which we operate is the traditional territory of many nations, including the Mississaugas of the Credit, the Anishnabeg, the Chippewa, the Haudenosaunee, and the Wendat peoples. We recognize the enduring presence of many diverse First Nations, Inuit, and Métis peoples and are grateful for the opportunity to meet and work on this territory.

Book*hug Press

To love. To be loved. To never forget your own insignificance.
To never get used to the unspeakable violence and the vulgar
disparity of life around you. To seek joy in the saddest places.
To pursue beauty to its lair. To never simplify what is complicated
or complicate what is simple. To respect strength, never power.
Above all, to watch. To try and understand. To never look away.
And never, never to forget.

—Arundhati Roy, *The Cost of Living*

CONTENTS

INTRODUCTION

Some years ago, I found myself on a farm near the border of California. It was late June and drought had fully set in. The grounds were bone dry; the clearing by the barn had no grass left. Up on the distant hills, you could see where previous fires had burned swaths of the forest away: large patches of brown amidst the verdant green. I was there for a weeklong retreat that was part environmental action, part spiritual practice, and they gathered us in a circle once everyone arrived. *We are in fire season,* our hosts explained, dust rising from the cracked earth between us. *If a forest fire begins, we will ring the farm bell continuously.* And then we'd have to run, they told us, back to the clearing to grab shovels from a pile. Before the flames could spread, we'd have to head toward them, and dig a trench deep and wide enough to keep the fire at bay.

The instructions alarmed me. *Who runs toward a fire?* Without training, without protection, without water. But around the circle, people were nodding. This is how most forest fires are contained: not with water, but with trenches. And deep in those drought lands, on that arid farm—a place used as a queer hospice, during the early years of the HIV/AIDS pandemic—we were hours from a fire station. There were no experts, no fire trucks, no beacons of safety nearby. Our best chance was one another; our best chance was to face the emergency with what we had, and to run—not right into the flames—but toward them.

This book is my effort to turn toward the fire. The trenches take all of us to dig; we each have a role to play. I may live with too much chronic pain to lift a literal shovel, to move earth with my arthritic hands, but the fire bell is ringing and this is what I can offer, so I do. I make an offering of this life, the memory and meaning that I carry, the research I've trained to do. I join my voice to the bell, head toward the rising heat. There is no perfect offering, I'm learning. No hero, no single protagonist. There is relationship. Kinship, estrangement, and entanglement with one another, with water and its absence, with the earth turned tinder and smoke rising through air.

RECENTLY, WHAT WE are facing has been called the Anthropocene—a new geological epoch, characterized by human intervention. The previous age, the Holocene, is marked by the melting of the polar ice caps nearly twelve thousand years ago. Before that, the Pleistocene—the *Ice Age*—lasted for around 2.5 million years. There is a natural widening of the earth's orbit and a tilting of its axis that shifts how solar radiation lands on the planet. It's believed this causes ocean warming and increased carbon dioxide levels, resulting in mass extinctions and the rise and fall of glacial ages. But this process takes place in deep-time, over tens of thousands to millions of years. In contrast, the timeline of an Anthropocene is staggeringly quick; it's often attributed to the last century, the "Great Acceleration," where human activity has surged across the planet. There is now enough concrete on the surface of earth to lay a thin crust around the entire planet. Our plastic has reshaped global landscapes, ocean systems, and the very fabric of our bodies—now riddled with microplastics. The imprint of grocery bags will remain for millennia, and it's been suggested we are in the "Plasticene"—an age of plastic—not the Anthropocene.

Wherever researchers begin, most agree that humanity crossed an irrevocable line when we split the atom in 1932. In the decades that followed, isotopes from the testing of nuclear weapons, waste from reactors, the devastation in Hiroshima and Nagasaki: these are marks of something entirely new on earth, life cut and remade by human hands, indelibly imprinted on the planet. Marks, thumbprints of innovation—also known as violence, war—an Atomic age, a Nuclearocene.

This collection contemplates a more expansive timeline—and explores a different sense of *us*, as well: not as a singular force in a human-centred world, but as multiple forces with divergent tools, only some of which built this fire. Ice cores extracted from Antarctica carry a record of atmospheric change, and these point toward the early 1600s—the global advent of European colonialism and slavery—as the threshold of the Anthropocene.[1] Our current environmental crisis can be traced in these records, through stone and ice, etymology and illness, pathogens and invasive species, back to the onset of colonial violence. Violence that continues; occupation that carries on. So perhaps we don't need a new name for this epoch at all, but rather an increase in widespread comprehension that the climate crisis we face is a crisis of colonialism.

From my vantage point—limited and biased by white-settler privilege—I am not trying to pin down a singular name for this era. The luxury and the challenge of these essays is to study the patterns, uncertainties, and intimacies between us. I come back to the term Anthropocene because it's part of the public lexicon— it's the main story being told—and I think those stories matter. Stories are a fundamental part of global systems; they not only interpret and define world change, they create it. The splitting of the atom began with a sequence of numbers, a theory, a conversation. The Anthropocene is a framework that can and will lead to research, funding, and policy; the idea carries geological weight. To me, what does seem fitting about the term is that it's personal and self-reflexive. Like anthropology or anthropomorphism, its bias is easy to find. The word points at us as we point toward it. It doesn't let the mirror disappear into a landscape of plastic bags and isotopes.

THE THRESHOLD OF an epoch is measured by geological change and widespread impact on the fossil record. Our plastic and tailing ponds—they leave an indelible mark. But records of world change are also—and mostly—living ones. Living records carried in each one of our bodies, our families, our stories, our lives. My ancestors live on in me through blood, through harm, through knowledge and responsibility. I come back to this fact and anchor my work here. What I want to bring to this conversation of world change is not *discovery*—a doctrine itself entangled with colonialism; I want to bring what each person carries: my own thumbprint of this crisis, my own way to turn toward the fire. There are infinite variations, and that's what we need, I think—that's what ecosystems call for to function: variation, contrast, divergence, multiplicity. There are no singularities or straight lines in nature; no heroes, no hierarchies in the forest. There is a deep understory; a mycorrhizal, fungal network that runs beneath the trees, tiny threads of mycelium that connect individual plants, transferring water, carbon, nutrients, and knowledge.

I've worked to reflect environmental patterns and non-human relationships in the structure of this book. Each section contemplates intimacy and entanglement with a different element: earth, fire, water, air, and finally *spirit*, or what others might call *ether* or mystery; the aspect of our world that is not tangible through the senses. A sixth section, The Understory, acts like the understory of a forest. Companion essays, additional research, and contemplations can be found there. This section can be turned to throughout the book, or at the end. This circular, elemental form was a way to contemplate the Anthropocene without prioritizing progress or human structures. This form also reflects how I relate to this world. In my Irish and Italian ancestral lines, and in the Reclaiming witchcraft tradition I am part of—a tradition of witchcraft that grew, in many ways, out of anti-nuclear protests in the Bay Area in the 1980s—there is a practice of turning toward these elements one at a time. To say, basically: *hello* and *thank you*; to deepen both relationship and responsibility to this world.

"Our body is a community," Thich Nhat Hanh once wrote. "The trillions of non-human cells in our body are even more numerous than the human cells. Without them, we could not be here in this moment." Interconnection is at the heart of our reality—that's what I believe. And that's where this book begins: reckoning with an epoch of interconnection and interdependence. Not as an era than can be given a singular name, not as a context that exists beyond my body and choices, but as a web of life to which I belong, as a road I am driving down, as a fireline of history that is still burning in the forest around me.

AS I WROTE this book, the pandemic began—a new threshold of interconnection; the immune systems of the world instantly bound to one another. The news kept saying: *Imminent threat, imminent risk.* And I kept thinking of the geyser I once saw in Iceland: how it kept blowing up, rising to the sky every few minutes in a shock of water and smoke. How we all stood around it: watching, waiting for it to hit again. There was no set pattern; you couldn't say how long it would take to explode. So, everyone just stood there with their cameras, recording the slow moment of water over rock, slushing around this hole that went toward the centre of the earth. We knew it was coming, but there was no preparing for the shock. Every time, we gasped.

Imminent threat, imminent risk. The words kept coming up, more than ever before. I had already named this book *Imminent Domains*; I had already planned to write about illness, uncertainty, and change. My life had been torn apart by Lyme disease; I knew something of zoonotic illness, loss, and adaptation. At least I thought I did. But COVID-19 was a reckoning of interdependence—a sign of how intimately we are bound to one another. And, paradoxically, the most profound isolation our world has known. By spring, I was facing long COVID, a significant concussion, and isolating alone. I felt grief-stricken for the world. And due to my concussion, my right pupil went slightly out of alignment with my left. It was like I saw a different world through each eye. Through my left: the world as it had been. Through my right: a new reality. I couldn't write like that—I could barely walk from the vertigo it caused. To write this book, I had to learn to see again—to see in a new way—with one eye on the past, and one eye on the present.

My pupil didn't right itself; instead, my brain learned to compensate for the divergence. I know it's there and I still feel it sometimes—a sudden disorientation, a spin to the world, one eye flashing in pain. Even as I write this, spots and distortions are rising in that eye, and I'm reminded of the bridge in my vision—the place where time converges, where loss meets adaptation. I'm reminded, as well, of the gaps in what I can see—lacunas that my experience of the world will never comprehend. Sometimes, *lacuna* means unfilled space or interval, sometimes it means the missing portion of a book or manuscript. And beneath these essays there is a deep contemplation of what cannot be known. By me, specifically. And by us, collectively, in the midst of this changing world.

When I was learning to see again, I turned off the news. I lay on a blanket on the grass and studied the sky instead. I sat in the yard with my imminent body, full of risk and change and threat. To love this world is not a simple thing. But no matter what you do, life happens. That's the funny, forgivable thing about the earth. It is not only loss that is imminent: it's creation. For months, I lay on that grass. And in June, cicadas that had been hibernating for seventeen years finally broke free. They sang through dusk, right to dawn. And it's their chirping that brought me back to language. Their shiny green bodies, and that ongoing song.

KEYSTONE ECOTONES

(earth)

Life finds a way.

—Dr. Ian Malcolm (Jeff Goldblum), *Jurassic Park*

DEFORESTATION

WHEN THE TICK bit me, I was lying in a field. It was August, a clean, hot month. The nights on the farm were cool with air blowing in from the nearby ocean. In the mornings, fog hung over the fields. But by midday, the sun would dry it all bare: the dew in my hair, the crops, the fogged windowpanes in the farm kitchen, where I was earning my keep as a cook. When I could, I would lie down in the orchards and fields alone and simply watch what was above me: sky, leaf, ripening apple. That's what I was doing when it happened: resting on the earth in a blue cotton slip. My hair woven into the grass, my bare legs stretched out like a canvas for sun and insects. I'd never heard of Lyme disease. I thought the worst thing that could bite me was a spider. I didn't even know that ticks existed when one climbed down my dress and bit me on my breast.

It was the most intimacy I'd had in months. I'd left Montreal behind me, and the bars, and the men and women I'd been dating, and every dress I owned except that old cotton shift. I'd left it all behind me, like a woman breaking up with her life and her body, to try and stretch my pain away with meditation and yoga, and sobriety and abstinence and nature, all at once. On that farm, I just had to cook porridge for the community at the break of dawn, watch men roll hay in the fields, and try to forget the rest of the world. At least that was the plan. Sometimes it seemed like it was working: like a sugar craving, my old life—the life of two months ago—would pass from my mind, from my body, and I would feel like the oats in my hand were the most important thing. I'd feel like all I needed was a tent and an air mattress to make my life work. Which was good, because that's what I had: a tent in the forest at the back of the property, and an air mattress that deflated each night.

I was learning to love even my crappy air mattress through the power of not-complaining. *Rise above!* it said on T-shirts at the market in town. *Let that shit go!* I wanted to rise above the pain I'd been living—pain that might be complex PTSD, or just *not trying hard enough*; pain that could be bipolar depression, or *possibly just candida*? Flowers grew from the compost heap in the orchard. I wanted my life to be like that, so I quit sugar and flour. I stopped speaking about the problems I saw—in my health, and in my community. I walked barefoot across the wet field every morning, and practised gratitude. I studied the deer in the orchard, and practised gratitude. *It's just a spider bite*, I told myself, when I looked in the mirror. *Stop being so sensitive*, I added, like a shitty ex-boyfriend to myself.

Silence could not make the problem go away. Instead, it made it worse. The mark persisted and a red circle rash formed around it—an *erythema migrans*—a clear sign of Lyme disease. But I didn't have a partner, a close friend, or a doctor to ask for advice. So even as I grew feverish and lethargic, I repeated the mantras I had recently learned: *Illness is a state of mind. Complaining only makes pain worse.* I took colloidal silver and spirulina, like everyone else on the island. I fasted and studied the deer. I blamed myself for my exhaustion and tried to push through.

Except, there was no *pushing through.* There was an ecosystem within me, and it had just begun to bloom.

WE ARE LIVING in an age of zoonosis. Governance, global health, and the world market: they are tied, in blood and in breath, to diseases that can travel between animals and humans. Coronaviruses have shown us this, emerging as diseases through animal-to-human, zoonotic transmission.[1] Where we meet, where we encounter each other: the entire world hinges. A personal future veers sharply. A collective reality arises that may look nothing like five minutes ago.

The deer on the farm, eating roses in the orchard: they looked so gentle, like they could do no harm. But the opposite was true. The deer had overpopulated the island. They lived with hardly any predators: the wolves were all gone, and only a few cougars and bears were left to hunt them. Those deer ate the fields to stone and the gardens to stem, and many carried the spirochete of Lyme disease within them. *Borrelia burgdorferi*, the bacteria behind the illness, does not harm their species. The same is true of field mice, and other small mammals. In the orchard, in the field: ticks latch on to them and acquire the Lyme spirochete. Those ticks then become carriers; catalysts able to pass the bacteria on to the next animal they bite. An animal like me, in my blue summer dress, resting my naked skin in their habitat.

The tick that bit me had likely first bitten a deer. So really, it is where the deer and I met, where our blood touched and mingled that matters. It's the deer that entered my life and turned my health like a garden to stone. *B. burgdorferi*, that spirochete, that smart bacteria that causes no harm to its original host: in me it replicated, formed biofilms, became dormant for years. Until eventually—years from that field—I became sick in a way that could not be ignored: chronic pain, chronic fatigue, neurological problems, heart arrhythmias, and a migraine each day. My blood tests still came back normal, showing only a dramatic rise in white blood cells: I was fighting some kind of infection—of what it was uncertain. It was only then I remembered my blue dress in August, the hayfield, the mark on my breast. And the *erythema migrans*, the red circle rash that expanded around it, like a bull's eye of illness; like a beacon of climate change.

ACCORDING TO THE Centers for Disease Control and Prevention, three out of four emergent infectious diseases will arise from zoonosis; six out of ten existing diseases already have.[2] Lyme disease is a form of zoonosis passed through a vector—the tick—and it cannot be passed between humans, so it poses a somewhat individualized risk. But Lyme transmission, like malaria and other vector-borne illnesses, is rising dramatically as habitats are decimated and climates destabilize and warm. I have contracted all three—COVID-19, Lyme disease, and malaria—so I know it's not a question of one disease versus another. They can converge and overlap like animals and insects do in any forest.

In the context of the pandemic, my afternoon in the field feels almost peaceful. The sunlight, blue cotton, deer eating roses. My body falling into a sick bed of autoimmunity for so many years: it can be described in watercolour. The slight green lake and knotted brown trees, the forest where I slept peacefully while the pathogen grew within me. Truly, there is something relatively gentle about a vector-borne illness like Lyme: you cannot give it to anyone else. The encounter is between you and nature directly; your body, insects, grass, and deer. Sick with COVID-19 at the onset of the pandemic, I discovered how much this mattered. I discovered the mercy of Lyme was that I was an incubator for myself alone. I had done no accidental damage, no unwitting harm to others.

Only, it is not that simple. Zoonotic disease can never be a closed circuit that belongs to one body alone. It is an illness of relationship, disease formed in the place where we meet. No positive thinking, no *rising above* can change that. No antibiotics can eradicate the root cause in an ecosystem, only treat the spirochetes of Lyme alongside our healthy bacteria, eradicating both with no differentiation, until everything is gone. Leaving the gut, like an old growth forest, clear-cut.

THE FIRST DOCUMENTED research into Lyme disease took place in Lyme, Connecticut, in the 1970s, by the Yale School of Medicine. At the time, individuals in the town had become sick with symptoms that matched those of rheumatoid arthritis: swollen joints, pain, and fatigue. But they also had neurological symptoms and a bull's eye rash that no doctor could explain. In 1982, ticks were finally identified to be the vector of transmission, by a scientist studying Rocky Mountain spotted fever. This discovery not only clarified the source of the illness, it explained why certain communities were so impacted. The disease was spreading in towns that had been built into forest edges; it was rising where deforestation had recently taken place, causing ticks to proliferate. Developers were building vacation homes on the beach in Connecticut, and townhouses right into the national park in Massachusetts. Natural habitats had become backyards, and they were filled with deer, field mice, and foxes.

This is where zoonosis thrives: in the gentrification of forests, in the hunger of wild species driven together, driven toward us, by drought and deforestation. It thrives where insects thrive, and insects thrive where temperatures rise. Zoonosis flourishes in summer vacations taken to the coast, running barefoot through the grass and sand—and then it expands to any ankle it can find. We reach a hand toward nature and it reaches back, offering an intimacy through illness we never expected, and never wanted to find.

The illnesses we discover are not always new. Because of the sudden bouts of illness in the 1970s, and the timeline of Yale's research, Lyme was speculated to be an emergent infectious disease of the last century, one that had developed regionally and reflected biological, evolutionary changes in the bacteria, the tick, or both. But in 2017, a research team from Yale sequenced the genome of the largest-ever collection of ticks, and identified *Borrelia burgdorferi* as an ancient bacteria, existing for at least sixty thousand years in multiple ecosystems. They concluded: "The recent emergence of human Lyme disease likely reflects ecological change—climate change and land use changes over the last century—rather than evolutionary change of the bacterium."[3]

In other words, the citizens of Lyme, Connecticut, did not fall sick with a new disease; they fell sick with a new relationship. Specifically, many of them fell sick with trophic impact of their own settler colonialism—just as I eventually did.

Biodiversity has a dilution effect on the spread of disease. With an abundance of space, biodiversity and variation between species, there was far less concentration of the Lyme spirochete, and as such, far less chance it would be transmitted to humans. But the clearcutting of forests for colonial settlement and resource extraction, coupled with targeted hunting of keystone predator species, led to a "population explosion of white-tailed deer," the expansion of ticks into new landscapes, and the chances those ticks would carry disease.[4]

Throughout the last century, these patterns of deforestation and overpopulation have only increased. Tick populations have also risen dramatically due to warming climates, reinforcing the spread of the spirochete and increasing the possibility of its transmission. Simultaneously, we've expanded development toward them. Into this growing hotbed of bacteria, we've built our homes. Right into the forest edges, closer and closer to more and more ticks, we've *selfied*.

I didn't just lay myself in a hay field; I lay myself at a crossroads.

AT THIS CROSSROADS: the more species diversity we lose, the more distilled bacteria and viruses become, and the more we are at risk of zoonotic disease. When species simultaneously face habitat loss, overpopulation and overcrowding, circumstances are primed for transmission within and between wildlife species, and the creation of variants that are then able to cross the zoonotic line to humans. (For more on this, see companion piece in The Understory: "On Zoonotic Disease and Global Health," page 195).

In February 2021, the director-general of the World Health Organization (WHO), Dr. Tedros Adhanom Ghebreyesus, spoke to this, stating: "The COVID-19 pandemic is a powerful demonstration that the health of humans, animals and ecosystems is intimately linked …. We cannot protect human health without considering the impact of human activities that disrupt ecosystems, encroach on habitats, and further drive climate change."[5]

Likewise, the Wildlife Conservation Society (WCS) compiled a literature review for eight different zoonotic illnesses in 2020, including Lyme, malaria, SARS, and COVID-19. Drawing from diverse research sources, they concluded: "More zoonotic diseases are found in threatened species facing declines in their habitat, or high pressure from exploitation, compared to those threatened for other reasons."[6]

The WCS report made specific recommendations, in alignment with the "One Health" framework—a framework promoted by the United Nations and the World Health Organization—including Indigenous leadership in the preservation of ecosystem integrity, particularly where biodiversity and ecosystems currently remain intact. But as I write this in late July 2021, Indigenous land defenders and protestors are being arrested at the Ada'itsx/Fairy Creek watershed, facing off against logging of one of the final stands of old growth forest in the region. These circumstances are only one example of the ongoing ricochets of state violence—just the largest show of force this month—amidst years of Royal Canadian Mounted Police (RCMP) action against land and water defenders. (For more on this, see The Understory: "On RCMP Violence: A Note," page 199.)

This is more than a paradox; it's a paradigm. Armed RCMP officers in helicopters sky-lift protestors from trees, as I write this. A government task forces analyzes how to prevent the future spread of zoonotic disease, as I write this. I stare out my mother's window, at the tree in her yard that will soon get torn down for condos. It has been growing there since I was born. It is just one tree, out-side of one settler's window—and still, it feels devastating. Today, my three-year-old goddaughter will be carried by her mother, seventeen kilometres on foot, up past the RCMP barricades at Ada'itsx. Her mother called last night, and my chronic fever rose as we spoke; an echo of zoonosis, and a constant reminder that climate change is not just around us, it is within us.

THIS IS HOW I understand it now: my body never left that field. I am still there, even now, my blood touching the memory of a deer as the sun warms the grass beneath me. That summer was the first time I felt like I lived in intimacy with nature. And I was right: every cell in my being was tuning to the ecosystem, to the dirt. But my joy, my love, my wonder at being part of it, could not make it a good relationship. My lineage is not one of symbiosis. I wanted to live so close to the deer that they woke me eating the wild crocuses by my tent. But we did not belong together. Our lives, our blood, were not meant to touch in this proximity. Only in an ecosystem out of balance could our bodies infinitely kiss.

A decade into this journey, I've come to see my tick bite as a catalyst. I may never know whether the chronic pain and illness were already dormant within me, waiting for a reason—for a bite, for a fever—to rise to the surface, or if they began with that infection. But I do know we can't simply—*Rise above! Let that shit go!*—when it comes to the ecosystems between us. Silence could not prevent the rough touch of climate change or my tick bite turning to disease. When I left Montreal, I could leave the bars and the dresses and the booze, but not the fact of being human. Not the exquisite and painful truth that I am part of this world; this world that is both united and divided by zoonosis. We are part of an ecosystem—kin to each other, and kin to species beyond us. Desire cannot remove us from this biological web; from the entanglement of our blood and breath with illness, with insects and animals, with one another. When it comes to infectious disease, the choices we make are choices for each other.

We have to begin with ourselves—what I have is this one reckoned body—but there are systems within us; we aren't so alone in that. Illness is not a personal failing, whatever the internet suggests. Where we meet disease, we meet the world. We touch the felled trees and the warming climate when the tick touches us. We contract, in our lungs, the forced proximity of misaligned species that gives rise to infectious disease. And for some of us, that meeting—that encounter, that joining together—it never ends. Our bodies, our lives, become a new thing altogether. We live with the tick, the mosquito, the vector, in a bond beyond marriage, in a bond with ourselves. History meets policy and policy meets blood—it's the Anthropocene that crawls down my dress, in that hayfield in August. The sun high and bright, the tick and I meeting without realizing we may never part in this lifetime. Our encounter both ancient and sudden; echoing between species, between systems, through time.

REWILDING

What might happen if you could summon back into the mouth what also should be summoned back into the landscape?

—Robert MacFarlane, "Speaking the Anthropocene"

ITTING ON A pink couch, alone in your one-bedroom apartment, you start crying over a YouTube video of wolves. It's a deep, slow cry where the tears simply roll down your face. *You are being ridiculous,* you tell yourself, *get it together.* But instead, you press refresh on the video *How Wolves Change Rivers,* and lean into the couch as the packs start howling.

The wolves had been gone from Yellowstone for seventy years, the narrator George Monbiot explains, before they were reintroduced in 1995. Without predators, elk had grazed the hills to stone. But the return of the wolves kept the herds out of the valleys, and the land re-greened, regenerated. Trees shot up, migratory birds landed, beavers built dams that brought fish. Hawks, eagles, and ravens returned to eat scraps left by the wolves. "Then the rivers changed," he explains. The tree roots stabilized the banks, changing the shape and course of the rivers. "The wolves," he says, "transformed not just the ecosystem but the physical geography."

You want your body to be a river, then. No longer this ill and exhausted landscape, but a part of the wilderness: altered, adapted, a thing that runs clean. You picture yourself starfished on the bank, cold water flushing over you, through you, until you are part of it. Your pain and grief absorbed, dissolved, and moving clean through Yellowstone. Like a film on fast-forward, you see the clouds seize and dance, watch algae fornicate on your bank, the belligerent green sprouting. Days blink into years and you witness the rewilding of the canyon.

A minute later, you open your eyes. There's a YouTube ad playing and it's cold in your apartment. You can't will your body into a river; that's the truth of it. There's no unmaking your humanity, no changing your relationship to illness or ecology by staring at the internet. If some part of you can heal, recover—rewild even, like that canyon—you need to find something to do the work of those wolves.

•

IN EVERY ARC there is a keystone. This stone is under the least pressure and yet, the whole structure would collapse without it. Sixty years ago, a zoologist named Robert T. Paine studied a constellation of starfish until he concluded the animal kingdom functioned the same way. He coined the phrase *keystone species.*

A species whose removal or return could shift an entire ecosystem. It's mine that I'm after.

·

> **re·wild** *verb* | gerund or present participle: rewilding. Restore (an area of land) to its natural uncultivated state (used esp. with reference to the reintroduction of species of wild animal that have been driven out or exterminated). EXAMPLE: "Talk of rewilding North America gives some people nightmares of wolves running through the streets of Chicago and of grizzlies in LA." (*Oxford Dictionaries*)

ARE YOU PICTURING wolves on your sidewalk now? Imagining brown bears at the side of your home? Or maybe, just distracted by my use of *you*? Like we know each other or something, like I'm sitting beside you on the couch. *You* didn't cry through that film (or did you? Maybe you paused reading, looked it up, and wept like I did). And here I am, addressing you as in *you*, after addressing you as in *me*. The perspective shouldn't be mutable, and yet I keep feeling like it is: my senses mix, the pronouns shift, and what is linear drops away.

I know this could be clearer, just like I know I'm not supposed to address you directly, but I'm wondering if this is part of the keystone I'm seeking: finding a new way to tell a story, admitting the relationship between us. You there, on the other side of the page. Me here, snatching definitions of *the wild* off the internet. I want to invite you in. I want to admit the instability of my perspective, how mutable and subjective it is. Subjective, biased by privilege, and changing all the time. I am looking for the places we meet, where we tangle together, though there may be no *we* between us. Each of us arrives to a book, to a story, to language, with our own relationship to power and privilege, to loss and to land, and I do not know how you arrive here.

I arrive here like I arrive to all questions of ecology: aligned by my ancestry, citizenship, and the framework of my upbringing, with the control and extraction of resources. I am who the wolves were shot for, I am a descendant of those shotguns. My grief for the wolves, for the eroded riverbank, is real—lying for days, immobilized, on my pink couch—but mine is a certain type of hunter's grief; his loneliness as he retrieves the body of the cub he's just felled, only to picture it rising again, miraculously, to race across the field.

And *you?* I wonder, I lean into the question. I keep trying to erase the word *we* as I write it, and still it comes up, a sign of my bias, but also an echo—an ongoing, ringing bell—of interconnection, of the forces that bind us together.

No single person creates a language. All words, and all stories, are built through collaboration. Collaboration between humans, between the animate and inanimate, the seen and unseen. Between species, even, as we give names to what moves around us. I come back to this fact; I anchor my work here. I look around the room, I look out my window. I trace where my life meets the treeline, or the absence of a forest. Words are my work in this world, and language seems like a good place for my questions to begin.

OXFORD SUGGESTS *WE* are afraid of rewilding. It says *some people*, at least. Why contextualize the concept within a nightmare? Behind this definition, I imagine a room of shadowy figures in Oxford, England, wearing Oxford blazers and Oxford shoes, and I get why these men are scared. Who needs a dictionary when there might be a grizzly around the corner? What is precise language to an imminent cougar attack?

Our current world structure relies heavily on singularities and definition. Industrialization and capitalism have required precise, agreed-upon language. How else could we build cities, govern countries, sign international trade agreements? We've needed an immutable, fixed point. Something to act as bricks as we built this world.

Our relationships to government, to the jobs we hold, to the lands we are on—stolen, occupied lands on Turtle Island—are formalized and mechanized (even: weaponized) through this precise language in contracts. Contracts that say *this* will be *this* and only *this*. But even in a settler-state framework, if you look at insurance contracts, there is often a clause: *except for an Act of God*. Flood, hurricane, earthquake. *This* is *this* until nature says otherwise. Our language is our language until nature renders it irrelevant, and then meaning shifts.

Is this the real nightmare Oxford is referring to? A world where the fixed point of language breaks, where the boundaries of life aren't so clear. Already, they are letting words drop from some of their children's dictionaries, like a pre-emptive strike. *These words have fallen into disuse,* they tell us. But maybe it's more that an English dictionary cannot contain an object in motion—nature in the arch of uncertain extinction or return—and so it's best to leave it out of the record; to leave it to the stillness and certainty of the past. *Obsolete,* the dictionary says, erasing *acorn* before the seed can finish falling to the earth.

I HAVE NEVER had nightmares of rewilding. What always scared me was obsolescence and our level of control. As a child, I had dreams of a nuclear spring on a regular basis. My third-grade class folded one thousand paper cranes; I read about Hiroshima. I wondered why my family didn't have access to a bomb shelter, and in its absence created one for myself in my sleep. The Cold War had just ended in 1989, and nothing frightened me as much as the atom bomb; the fact that our world had the capacity to utterly and completely obliterate itself. I believed we would one day use this capacity. That our world would delete itself as a series of red buttons were pushed. The future I saw after this left no room for regeneration. Everything was flat, grey, and silent. There was no seed of life left. In the world I pictured, there wasn't even wind.

This fear of an *end place*, an edge of the world we could fall from, has left me immobilized in the past. At the far end of panic attacks, you can become completely catatonic. Rather than breathing quickly and gasping for air, in this state you can feel unable to breathe, move your limbs, or speak. For me, this feels like sitting at the bottom of a muddy lake. And once I am there, gravity tells me to stay; let the water have its way with me, let silence and fear do what it will. *I should be afraid*, instinct tells me. *Look at all these things I have to be afraid of.* It is excruciating to return to the shore. To begin to move and breathe, to think and speak again.

I have spent a great deal of time avoiding this feeling, this bottom of the lake. I remember, years ago, trying to convince my mother to be more optimistic. "No, you're wrong," my mother responded. "I'm sorry, but you are. Everything is dying. It's different this time. All the scientists I read are agreeing. The damage we are doing is permanent, it's irreversible. Forever."

I tried to respond: "Think back longer. You know the Rockies—they were once underwater. Think back past the dinosaurs, Mom.

Imagine how small we are, how short our life span is compared to the ocean. This world will go on, no matter what." But I couldn't find the words. Instead I burst into tears, told her she was unsupportive, and slammed the door to my room, like I was still sixteen. Until I faced my mother with my beliefs scrawled like a kindergarten art piece, expecting her applause, I hadn't realized how much I was relying on this faith, or how truly shaky it was. I was asking her, quite literally, to believe in life after death. And I wanted her to perform the act like it was a duty of motherhood. To clap and smile, say: *You're right!* To see what I couldn't yet: that my belief was not only an experience of the world, but a strategy for surviving it.

We live on a precipice of complete environmental collapse. We know, at least conceptually, what this could mean for us. A loss of our current way of life—maybe even the ground beneath our feet, shaken, split open by an earthquake. We live—differently and yet collectively—in relationship to this loss. *Everything could die.* How can we grieve a loss that spans our entire existence?

I once looked up Kübler-Ross's model of grief and tried to pin myself against it. I thought maybe I could understand the state of the world through the categories of an expert: denial, anger, bargaining, depression, acceptance. *Yes,* I thought, with every category I read. *That sounds about right.* I see those phases in me, I see them in my surroundings. We disassociate, ignore, then lash out in the wrong places. Just look how I treated my mother: *classic transference.* We try to barter the melting ice caps with riding our bikes to work, while the heads of state negotiate accords that may not make any difference. We are facing an epidemic of depression that continues to grow.

But when I arrived at the last stage, I realized the exercise was futile. How can we accept a thing we can't name? We don't know, that's the truth of it. This is not about climbing a ladder toward acceptance of a diagnosis that has been made for the world we live in. We are negotiating with a space of unknowing. And there, I catch myself. *Negotiate.* How do you negotiate with, quite literally, nothing? You are sitting at the table by yourself.

Maybe if I could press all these words together like they were the ingredients to make bread; if I could knead and bake these stages into one mass that slowly rises in the oven, that is always on the brink of collapse. But in Kübler-Ross's model, we progress through loss the way we walk through a house, entering room by room.

·

THERE IS A memory I turn over in my mind, all the time. It's a cold, clear day in April and I'm standing in a small studio at the Banff Centre. The room is carpeted and grey, but the front wall is clear glass, floor to ceiling. In front of me, mountains knuckle up into sky. Light leaks into the room, so bright I can't focus. I put down the poems I'm working on, stand at the glass, and I can almost taste the early spring through the window. That's when the wolf appears. She's an arm's breadth from the glass, sallow and hungry, the colour of old snow. She kneads the frozen earth, and I can't help but wonder how strong the windowpane is. I watch her put her snout to the earth, sniffing. I want her to look at me. The fur on her stomach is loose and caked with mud, she's half starved, I realize, and I don't want her to look at me anymore. That's when she does, of course; she turns and peers right into my small room. And we watch each other: just blinking and breathing, until she finally turns and pads away.

•

THE TRUTH IS, I didn't see the wolf. My friend Marla did, on the writer's retreat where I met her. She returned to the room where the rest of us were drinking and told us the story. I closed my eyes and listened, picturing myself there in that room. Then spent the next week in that studio, glancing up at the window, certain I'd catch sight of the wolf. I never did. But I have spent so much time with the memory that I have built my own relationship with it. I have lived in relationship to my own imagined encounter for ten years, and it has become a part of my life.

This is the closest I may ever get to a wolf. Some parts of nature we will only ever know through imagination and language. The relationship is still real, an aspect of our lives that operates in our choices and interactions. But it is abstract and mutable. How can we explain our relationship to the imagining of a thing? Maybe this is why we still visit zoos, even when we can see cruelty in them; we want the relationship to have a time stamp, a ticket, a context—even if our act of witnessing causes harm to the thing that we witness. Machu Picchu trampled under ten million feet; orcas dying in SeaWorld. Maybe the story doesn't feel real enough; maybe we want the encounter for good reason: to understand the animal inside ourselves by confronting another; to realize how small we are next to the vastness of a canyon. But often we are seeking revelations on nature at the cost of nature—at the cost of each other. And the more we do that, the more nature retreats. The earth quakes and laughs, floods and swallows; the more we find ourselves sitting at the table alone.

I RETURN, AGAIN and again, to this question: can the abstract be enough? Already, memory and language are all that remains of many species. Loss accumulates, extinctions quicken, and their names grow heavy with meaning. More and more, the abstract is what we have.

Here, I find myself turning to Annie Dillard: "Nature's silence is its one remark." She writes of a man on an island who is teaching a stone to speak—his practice an attempt to build a language, some verification, between himself and the unspeaking world. I cried on the bus when I read her essay for the first time. It was a crowded city bus, and I put on my sunglasses because people were staring. *Why I am even crying?* I asked myself, while crying, while thinking of the Yellowstone wolves. Is everything I do a negotiation of this silence? Have I been trying to make the stones around me speak?

If so, I am giving up the effort. *What is remembered lives,* we say in my tradition. Memory—that's how life carries on after death. Memory, imagination, art. We have to love what we cannot touch—that's what I'm learning. To survive, to collaborate, to surface from the bottom of the muddy lake or river: we need to bond with parts of the world we can't verify, can't speak to, can't understand. We need to care deeply for the profound unknown, and keen uncertainty between us.

"The silence is all there is," Dillard writes. "It is the alpha and the omega, it is God's brooding over the face of the waters; it is the blinded note of ten thousand things, the whine of wings." The stones are already speaking. That's what Dillard means, I think: the silence is their voice. And we cannot break that voice or own it, we cannot make it do our will. The unknown, the unspeaking, the un-languageable world: it is sacred. And when I listen to that silence, it can raise me from the bottom of the lake. It can carry me to shore.

•

THE KEYSTONE OF an arch stands at its apex. It is the last stone planted. It is what turns two outstretched angles into a bridge—a thing we can walk across. Everything else depends on this piece. We need it to sustain, to hold the other pieces in place.

Begin by listening, I tell myself. *Begin your stories here.* And into the space: a path, a gully—now a ravine—appears.

•

WHEN I WAS a kid, my mother would take me and my sister on walks to the only green space in our neighbourhood. We'd skip up the street, as the apartment buildings around us finally gave way to mansions that backed onto the ravine. She'd let us run off the path once we got there, then follow us into the sparse trees where we looked for frogs. We never found any. The only animal I found there as a child was the skeleton of a cat in a paisley duffle bag, under the bridge. I was nine. I never told anyone what I'd seen; tried to forget it. But the memory was always there: stark evidence of human cruelty, the cat clearly dropped from above, and I avoided those trees for years.

Back then, I didn't know how the ravine had formed, that water had once gushed through it. Toronto is a city of buried rivers: the so-called Garrison Creek and Humber River. But whether or not we remember this fact, the landscape does. Some years ago, the city flooded. In two hours, we received three months' worth of rain. Enough water so that cars were submerged on the parkway. A lawyer abandoned his Ferrari there, and climbed right out the window. Photographs of commuters wading through the highway were shown on the news, and pictures of Union Station, with crudely photoshopped alligators and sharks swimming through the tunnels. A GO Transit train thought it could make it, drove right into a newly formed lake. Thousands of passengers were stranded, shaking their heads: *Who thinks a train can run through water?*

That storm flooded through the ravine near my mother's house. Around midnight, after the rain had stopped, I took my book and sat on the porch. The power was out in the apartment building across the way, and the street was quiet. Just my front porch light and the near-full moon; no one around. I don't know what instinct told me to look up, but when I did, there was a fox in the centre of the street. Like a small, lithe dog with a pointed nose. I'd never seen a fox before. It paused, looked right at me, then continued on its way. Trotting down the street, under the glow of the streetlights, heading into town with a sense of purpose.

LAZARUS SPECIES

THERE IS A small wooden cupboard on my mother's front porch. It is worn by weather, and the drawer is filled with gardening gloves, flower cutters, and dried poppy stems that she gathers in spring. I found a card from my favourite childhood game, Endangered Species, in that drawer. The card is black and white, and there is a small bottle drawn on it with a skull and crossbones. The symbol means: *poison*; *toxic*. This was one of the ways your chosen species could die in the game. As you moved around the board, you encountered chance cards based on real threats: one card read *habitat loss*. Another read *poaching*. Others read *oil spill, contamination of land*.

We played the game often—after school and every weekend—but I never changed who I tried to save. I was always the black-footed ferret. I would rush my hand into the box and grab the player card quickly, as if my friends and family might compete for it. They never did. You could choose from the panda, or the sea otter, or the polar bear—species that were T-shirt-ready, species that showed up on ads for the World Wildlife Fund. But the ferret and I were bonded; all I wanted was to rescue it again and again.

In the bright spinning lights of the nineties, *global warming* was new language. I dreamed of a nuclear spring, and I also dreamed of an infinite summer. As if the sun would rise, and never stop rising, until there was no place left to belong. We planted trees in the yard at school, and celebrated Earth Day like it was a sabbath, and even our cartoons said the villain was *smog*. My family couldn't afford a car, but that was better for the earth anyway. We dug a hole in our aunt's backyard for compost and she filled it with worms. "This is how you make earth," she explained. Good clean earth out of garbage. That's what I wanted: not only survival, but resurrection. For the apple core to become the flower, for my nightmares to shift into dreams, for my efforts to equal survival.

I had little time off from my extinction anxiety. My best friend, I remember, dealt with hers by gathering pets. Every few months, her parents would allow her another, until her small basement bedroom held a turtle, a hamster, and a full tank of fish. She was always bringing the cat and dog down there too, so I'd come over and find her surrounded by five different species. Then her father would take us to McDonald's—the only restaurant in the budget—and we'd order a "cheeseburger, no meat please," which was just cheese and a pickle with ketchup. The staff always laughed at us, but we did it anyway, because there was a hole in the ozone layer and we had to save the earth. "There's only a slim chance," they told us, "that we can close that hole." I pictured it over us, just a raw hole the sun came through like a laser. The way you could set grass on fire with a magnifying glass; I pictured it like that, except we were the grass.

That notion never left me. How could it? But I learned to be more comfortable with the discomfort, with the fear and risk of it all, with the ongoing sense of an imminent disaster. The adults discussed ozone depletion over cigarettes in the kitchen, while we played Endangered Species in the carpeted living room. That's just how it was: there was only so much we knew about our present, let alone our future world.

SOMETIMES, I STILL picture the illustrated grasslands of Wyoming, as they were drawn in the game: prairie fields, sun-drenched. When I'm feeling hopeful, rain starts to fall in these visions. There's grass and snakes and rivers. Gone are the monocrop fields of canola and herds of commercial cattle, and instead there are prairie dog holes. The prairie dogs are burrowing beneath the earth, forming colonies and families. The prairie dogs are thriving, and there's a chance—small but real—that the black-footed ferret can too.

Like the grey wolves in Yellowstone, prairie dogs are a keystone species. They shape the landscape and survival of more than one hundred other species, including flora and fauna, predators and other prey. While keystone predators, like wolves and mountain lions, cause what is called a *top-down trophic cascade*—controlling overpopulation and maintaining species diversity—prairie dogs fill a different crucial role: they act as ecosystem engineers and shape the landscape around them, similar to the way beavers impact water systems.[1] Prairie dogs till and enrich the soil by burrowing holes and tunnels beneath it, increasing plant and insect life in their proximity, drawing pollinators and birds. Their dens become homes for swift foxes, snakes, and burrowing owls, and are the only known habitat of the black-footed ferret. They also make up 90 percent of the black-footed ferret's diet. So really, this is what my player card should have looked like: the ferret on one side, the prairie dog on the other.

What is a species without its environment? Without its keystone? The two are inextricably linked—almost like they are bees from the same hive. Or perhaps more like a snake that bites its own tail to form an infinite circle—except here it's a ferret, biting a prairie dog, who is digging a hole in the earth, that holds the ferret, that bites the prairie dog. If nature has a declarative truth, it's this: nothing survives on its own.

THE POISON CARD is all I have left of the game. A single playing card and memories—fragmented, but vivid—that pull me back and forth through time. In one, the black-footed ferret rises from a burrow on the Endangered Species card—alert, watching for threats. The sky is clear and bright. There are threats all around the ferret; threats in the hole in the earth it is rising from—poison, plague. The earth, the field around the ferret, is dry and barren, eaten to dust by commercial cattle. The sun pours down from what must be a hole in the ozone; the kind of hole coming for us all. *I'll save you,* I whisper, again and again, as I roll the dice. *This time we'll win.*

The game we are playing is supposed to be cooperative, but it's modelled after Monopoly. In Monopoly, you try to *own it all,* you try to bankrupt your sister across the room, you laugh as she goes to jail. In Endangered Species, you watch as your sister is the blue whale and the blue whale is *eliminated,* which you know means *dies*. And maybe you laugh, at first—maybe you even feel excited—but you also picture that shoreline in California where a whale recently beached. They could not get it back into the ocean, even when they tried to use a truck, then two trucks, and an excavator.

After you beat the whale, you beat your friend and her gorilla, and then you beat your friend's brother, Leo, who is an endangered whooping crane, and then you think of the Exxon Valdez oil spill—they are still cleaning it up—and the videos of black oil on all those cranes' wings, and that's how it happens: you win with the last crane folding its slick, black wings.

How does it feel to win? In your hand, the ferret rises triumphant from the prairie dog hole, like Lazarus, like a hero. Across from you, Leo's face turns red, and the crane card falls from his hand, and your sister starts shuffling the deck again, looking for a species with a better chance of survival. "Let's play together this time," she says—because you can also win as a group, by saving five species within one habitat; it's just you've never managed it—the game is rigged against it, no matter how hard you try. You look at your sister, she's your older sister, and she hasn't picked a new card after all. The whale is still in her hand, like that whale is still on that beach, melting to bone under the heat of the sun. "Okay," you say. "Try the sea turtle this time," you tell Leo. And you go back to the square marked Start. Because unlike an ecosystem, unlike the Arctic coast after Exxon Valdez, someone just needs to whisper, "let's try again," and you can clear the board and start from zero.

LIKE THE WOLVES in Yellowstone, prairie dogs in the Midwest did not simply vanish; they were systematically eradicated. These efforts began in the early 1900s and continued for decades as part of the ever-expanding colonial project to settle and convert ecosystems into agricultural land. Prairie dogs are antagonists to land development. They are nature's band of protestors: they reproduce widely and will dig tunnels beneath any development, ruining a field's ability to host crops or cattle—any cow that steps in their holes will easily break its leg. Farmers wanted them gone, developers wanted them gone—this was cattle country; this was oil-and-gas country—and so poison was spread down their holes, and shot guns were loaded, and shot guns were fired, and still more poison was poured right into their keystone tunnels. Flora, fauna, and the black-footed ferret: *DOA*.

Meanwhile, in those same burrows: zoonotic disease. The deadly sylvatic plague raged through the underground world, starting in the 1930s. The prairie dogs, with their complex, expansive family systems, died colony by colony, taken under by the new spread of disease, until they became a fragmented presence in the grasslands and plains. And joined with them—by blood and habitat, by behaviour and disease—the black-footed ferret died, too.

Unlike the prairie dog, the black-footed ferret was never abundant or populous. They are the only ferret species endemic to Turtle Island/North America—one of only three known species of ferrets in the world—and their role within ecosystems has always been unique, rare, and inimitable. In 1967, the black-footed ferret was placed on the first-ever endangered species list in the United States. There were only thirty-six species on the list, at that time. In 1973, the Endangered Species Act was passed into law, finally establishing actionable protection for the species on the list. But by then, no wild sightings of the ferrets had been reported for years. In 1979, the last mating pairs of black-footed ferrets died in captivity, and the species was officially declared extinct.

THE WHALE ON the beach in California. The crane, the seals, the gulls with black oil on their wings. *Save them!* I shout at my television, in memories of my childhood. A marine biologist looks back at me from the flickering screen, frowning. David Suzuki walks slowly through the forest, and talks in a low, sad voice. We watch a video about the clean-up of the Exxon Valdez spill, and a volunteer holds a gull over an indoor sink. She cleans the bird's wings with dish soap as it caws, and the oil rinses off, black down the drain, and the bird will survive—the bird will fly free. They've tagged its ankle. They'll follow its path into the distance, into the future; though maybe the gull will carry on forever and ever, never risk landing in an ocean again.

Our mother is a teacher, a brilliant teacher at a school down by the lake where she teaches kids our age. So she gives us more than the game; she gives us a picture book by Richard Bach called *There Is No Such Thing as Far Away,* full of watercolour paintings of gulls and owls. The animals are flying to visit a child on her birthday, and they tell the child they will always be with her, even if they can't be seen. My mother reads us other stories, too, one about reincarnation, another about selkies—women who become seals under full moons—Irish women like her. There may be death, but there is also life, and life *again.* Energy cannot be destroyed, the books teach us. What happens if you stand at the shoreline under a full moon? You can't know everything, and that makes life sweeter, easier to manage. Maybe the beached whale dies, but it also returns—and in my mind's eye, maybe it returns as a seal, as a selkie, and that selkie is also my mother.

My sister and I have never seen the ocean, except in documentary films, so this is how we begin to understand it: as a place of loss and shift, as memory and myth. A lake, except larger; a lake that goes on forever, just like those gulls flying on through infinite sky.

Don't look away, our mother is teaching us, from the violence or the beauty around you. If you close your eyes, you won't see either. So we don't look away, but we also don't look right at the sun. The first edition of Endangered Species was released in 1976, before the black-footed ferret was declared extinct. Fifteen years later, my sister and I were playing a beaten-up first edition of the game that hadn't been updated. And I was trying to rescue a species that had already fallen—fallen extinct, and then risen again.

"TAKE AWAY THE stone," Jesus says in the story of Lazarus. And so they take away the stone on the grave. "Lazarus, come out!" Jesus commands, and so the dead man emerges, wrapped in strips of linen. Two years after the black-footed ferret was declared extinct, it was found alive again in Meeteetse, Wyoming. From 1979 to 1981, its name existed beside the taxonomy of the dodo. And then, from the seeming black hole of nonexistence, it returned. It rose, like a miracle from the field, and landed in the muzzle of a ranch dog, who barked through the night, broke the ferret's back, and left it on the porch for his owners to find. Those ranchers brought it to a taxidermist, who knew what it was and called wildlife control. And when teams began looking, they found over a hundred. The ferrets weren't gone, after all—they had only been extinct to science, not the earth. And from then on, the black-footed ferret became known as a *Lazarus species*.

This is what *Lazarus taxonomy* means: there is a fossil record, then there is not—and then the record reappears. Like the echo imaging of a heart that is restarted. The printed line goes flat along the bottom of the page—and then, suddenly, it spikes again.

So it isn't, it turns out, only the bad things that are hidden from us. The unknowns are often terrible. But then, sometimes, they are a ferret rising undead from a prairie-dog hole. That first ferret—the one discovered by the dog in Meeteetse—is believed to a have been a scout. He was six miles away from the closest prairie dog hole, the only place black-footed ferrets can nest. So he was likely searching for a new habitat, and he led his species there: into the re-encounter, shared habitat, and ultimately, survival.

IN THE BIBLICAL story, Jesus says to his followers: "take off the grave clothes and let him go." But the telling seems to end there; it's a cliff hanger. The linens are unbound; the cage door is open, the bird flies free, the black-footed ferret is found on the porch. *And then what?* The child in me wants to cry, *and then what?* But there is no consistent answer. Some species return after brief absences and thrive, others reside in a purgatory of near-extinction for decades. The coelacanth—an ancient deep-sea fish—was thought to have gone extinct sixty-six million years ago, but has turned up at fish markets twice in the last century. The Aleutian cackling goose—a close relative of the Canada goose—was declared extinct in the 1920s, discovered again in 1962, and since then, it has rebounded so well it's basically a nuisance. But in contrast, after a century of dedicated searches and unconfirmed sightings, the ivory-billed woodpecker was once again declared extinct in fall 2021. "The *Lord God Bird* is dead," the *Washington Post* wrote alongside its obituary.[2] The bird was given that name, it's said, because the sight of it would make one shout out to the heavens.

Of the 112 black-footed ferrets found in Meeteetse, only eighteen survived by 1984. Those eighteen were brought into a captive breeding program. Their population fell to only seven—they came again to the very knife edge of extinction—before the ferrets began to successfully breed again. Thirty years after their reappearance, there are now more than seven hundred in existence; just over half in captivity, the rest spread across thirty reintroduction sites in North America. The risks they face are monumental, particularly because these ferrets have an extremely limited gene pool; they are all descendants of the final seven—except for one: Elizabeth Ann.

IN THE BIBLICAL story, Jesus has allowed for Lazarus' death, so that the miracle of resurrection might take place. "Do you believe this?" he asks, and then he calls forth the dead.

On December 10, 2020, Elizabeth Ann was born from cells that were cryo-preserved in the 1980s. This is the first time an endangered species in the United States has been successfully cloned. She is a clone of "Willa," one of the original Lazaruses captured in Meeteetse—but one who died without reproducing. So really, Elizabeth is the Lazarus of the Lazarus, the second-coming of the second-coming, rising from what we once called dead.

"Do you believe this?" I asked my mother, showing her a photograph of the newborn ferret resting in the gloved palm of the lead researcher, Ben Novak.

"Yes," she said simply, sipping her coffee, "I do."

I, on the otherhand, was *shook*. To be of the Endangered Species board-game generation is to be of the *Jurassic Park* generation. The exact, precise generation that saw the first film in the theatre before anyone spoiled the ending. I ran out when the velociraptors attacked, my mother trailing behind me. Cloning has always been a loaded concept, a place where fiction meets science, and I have rarely been inclined to trust it. So, I find myself troubled looking at pictures of slender Elizabeth Ann in Ben Novak's hand.

What are they to each other? Is he her god now? Is he her dad? He looks like a Hinge profile I might encounter if I lived close to his biotech company. He's clearly smiling behind the mask, behind his vaguely hipster glasses, and he holds the clone toward the camera as if it's a baby bird. That guy would *totally* call you the morning after. Why would you be threatened? By the potential future father of your children (I mean look at his kind eyes and job security), or, say, a theme park.

It's actually not a huge leap: Ben Novak to Jeff Goldblum as Dr. Ian Malcolm in *Jurassic Park*. The cloning of an endangered species is obviously not the same as the cloning of an extinct species, but Novak is part of an organization—Revive & Restore—that hopes to do both. In addition to working with Elizabeth Ann, Novak has been one of the lead researchers in a project that focuses on the passenger pigeon as a model candidate for de-extinction. Revive & Restore also developed a vision project, in connection with Harvard, exploring woolly mammoth revival. Their stated goal is to "enhance biodiversity through the genetic rescue of endangered and extinct species." Specifically, they promote the incorporation of biotechnology into standard conservation practice, and are at work on a genetic rescue toolkit that includes biobanking tools, gene-editing tools, and advanced reproductive technologies.[3]

"IT ALL SOUNDS LIKE *JURASSIC PARK*. HOW IS THIS DIFFERENT?" reads one question in the FAQ section of their website (*caps lock* theirs). They offer a solid response: "Real-world de-extinction is being conducted with total transparency. Eventual rewilding of a revived species can be no more commercial than the current worldwide protection of endangered species and wildlands. Ecotourism, of course, is a commercial activity often used to help fund the management of protected areas."[4]

They use so many of my favourite words in their answer. I could print out a page and erase the extant language until all I was left with was a poem: *revive, restore, return, rewild.* But "no more commercial" is not the same as zero commercial value. And the fundamental truth is this: there is no such thing as *de*-extinction. There is only the theoretical possibility of simulacrums, of "proxy" species, creatures born from the mixed genes of ancient animals (like the woolly mammoth) and their last remaining relatives (in this case, the Asian elephant).

The idea that an animal can come back from extinction might act as a buffer to our grief. It might suggest, as well, that protection and conservation are not as vital; not our last stand. But it is also scientific misnomer, basically a lie. Where two creatures from different eras meet, where their genes collide—who can say what the result would be, exactly? There are scientific estimates and philosophical arguments, and then there is *life*. There is the fact that we are, at best, proxies for the spark of creation. What we create is fabricated, manufactured, even when it is the stuff of life, and so—here's the catch—it can sometimes be treated like a commodity. Species brought back from extinction, and the methods used to enact Lazarus on the species, are potentially patentable by law.[5] And in light of this, both protection and restoration could have enormous financial outcomes, particularly when it comes to biobanks and patents. The laws and limits in this area are emergent, often only written as new discoveries and uses are found. Which seems risky, because we are discussing the most fraught area of bioethics: cloning, the cosplay of God.

ELIZABETH ANN WAS born into this liminal legal space, through a multiyear partnership between Revive & Restore, U.S. Fish and Wildlife Service, San Diego Zoo Global, the Association of Zoos and Aquariums, and the for-profit company ViaGen Pets & Equine; a cast of players that reads like *Jurassic Park* fan fiction. ViaGen's involvement was likely essential; the company holds three key patents for cloning technology—including the ones that gave us Dolly the sheep. But ViaGen's work also comes with a high level of controversy. Their slogan is *the worldwide leader in cloning the animals we love.* Click on the "initial cloning" button on their website and you'll find the steps and cost involved in cloning your pet —$50,000 USD for a dog, and $35,000 USD for a cat, paid in two equal instalments.[6] Famously, ViaGen is responsible for Barbra Streisand's two cloned dogs.

It is difficult for me to see how this kind of private cloning might contribute to a collective good. What are Barbra Streisand's dogs going to do for us, other than push medical ethics into a new frontier of complexity and media coverage? In other areas— medical research, conservation research—it is much easier to see an ethical justification for pushing the line. But the truth is, it's all mixed in: the money, the partners, the technology—and very little about this industry is transparent and clear. (For more on this, see The Understory: "On the Business of De-Extinction," page 213.) For example, the cofounder of Revive & Restore, Ryan Phelan, created one of the first direct-to-consumer DNA kits, and later sold that company and its genetic data to a pharmaceutical benefit manager.[7] And like Streisand's dogs, this fact makes me uneasy. With the widespread rise of personal genetic testing, concerns are regularly raised about bioethics, privacy, the risk of discrimination by health care companies, and the widespread lack of regulation.

Can we expect the sale of animal genome data to be better regulated than the sale of human data? What might genes-as-currency mean for Elizabeth Ann, Hinge-worthy Ben Novak, or the enormous biobank of extremely rare and vitally important genes that Revive & Restore is gathering with its "genetic rescue toolkit"? Where it is difficult to see who is behind the curtain, it is also difficult—if not impossible—to decide if you trust them, particularly with the cell-stuff of creation. These organizations may be guarding the very mitochondria of our survival. But how would we know? So, I come back to this question: What exactly does Revive & Restore mean by "total transparency?" Are they actually contrasting the honesty of the biotech industry with—direct quote—the "commercial secrecy of an island theme park."[8] Did *Jurassic Park* somehow set the bar on the ethics of de-extinction?

I want to trust those calling for restoration and rewilding. I agree with Revive & Restore's statement: "Ecosystems around the world face unparalleled biodiversity loss but solutions are available."[9] We need a wealth of solutions, including some that likely will challenge our sense of right and wrong. But can we trust that for-profit companies, working with organizations like Revive & Restore, will not patent what is patentable? They have to make their research and development money back somehow. And the birth of Elizabeth Ann is already entangled with the resurrection of Streisand's dogs.

WHO DO WE trust with the cosplay? How do we know we can trust them? Will Ben Novak be a good father/god/godfather to Elizabeth Ann and the litter of clones on its way? What about his bosses, their partners, and the money behind them? In an interview discussing the introduction of the cloned species to the wild line, scientist Dr. Samantha Wisely said to the *New York Times*: "It will be a slow, methodical process.... We need to make absolutely sure that we're not endangering the genetic lineage of black-footed ferrets by introducing this individual."[10]

What are the systems of accountability and oversight if they fail; if this does go awry? What if the reintroduction of Willa's genes through Elizabeth Ann inadvertently wipes out swathes of the remaining black-footed ferrets? This is being done—this entire process is being done—to preserve and expand the genetic diversity of the species, which theoretically will give it the best chance of adaptation and survival. I have been singing this tune—*the black-footed ferret must be saved, whatever it takes*—since I was seven. But once these genes are mixed—cloned with wild—they cannot be unmixed. You can't unring that bell.

This is where the story departs from any fantasy of *Jurassic Park*: We are talking about active ecosystems, productive landscapes; placing clones into the infinite interplay of wild species. We are talking about chaos—the chaos of nature—which makes it truly what it is: a thing beyond full recognition, that which cannot be completely divided, dissected, named, and known. It is in a constant state of evolution and change, and so science is in a constant state of discovery, only ever holding parts of the whole.

What do you call that *thing*, that unity, that un-languageable whole? I know it when I am silent, when I walk in a forest, or rest in a field. "It is the alpha and the omega," Annie Dillard says.

If you talk to a physicist, someone who deals with the incalculable, they might just call it *god*.

DEAR DR. KÜBLER-ROSS, I get it now. Here is the bargaining stage, at work in science: What would you trade, it asks us, for the survival of the black-footed ferret? Would you risk the patent? Would you risk pushing the bioethical line? What's better: the end of a species completely, or the end of that species' original wild line? And if the species can survive, the bargaining goes, maybe we can. Look into the mirror of death: see Ben Novak smiling at you. We can go to the brink, and we can *revive* and *restore*. We can return, since we cannot prevent. The bargain is: CRISPR gene editing or extinction. The bargain is: Elizabeth Ann doesn't exist without the profits of resurrecting rich people's pets. The bargain is: we do not know what we do not know of our future.

In the game of *Would You Rather* that I am playing with my personal god, I see the vast grasslands of Wyoming. There is a single black-footed ferret, on a single ranch, like the Lazarus found in Meeteetse. But this one is not a Lazarus; it's not a scout. It's the last wild ferret, the last black-footed ferret in existence. And it dies while I watch it. Under the drought sun, in those drought lands, unable to find shelter.

I don't look away from the vision; this is what it takes to weigh the question. What do I want for that ferret? What do I want for its kind? It comes to this: when I look into the mirror, I don't see Ben Novak. I see myself in the grasslands. Thirsty. The vastness of the sun becomes the only thing there is. What do I want? No extraordinary measures. Save the land around me; bring it water, richen its soil. But if I am the last of my kind, the final body: let me be. Let the enormity of grief that I am gone break like thunder.

You can't get me back once you've lost me, World; you can't whisper like children, "Let's try again," and start from zero. I choose DNR if I am on my last breath. Let that breath have its meaning. Impermanent, irreplaceable: let me join the wind.

MOUNTAINS THAT EAT MEN

(fire)

Many fires burn below the surface.

—Empedocles, 494 BCE, who is said to have
perished in the flames of Mount Etna

THE PLASTER CITIZENS
OF POMPEII

W E BROKE INTO Pompeii. Or more truthfully, we *snuck* into Pompeii. School buses were stationed in a parking lot and kids were standing around, laughing in big crowds. We couldn't afford tickets to get inside the ruins, but I wanted to see the city, I wanted to touch its history with my hands. The side entrance was for school groups and tour busses, it wasn't guarded. "Come on," I said to my partner. He looked around nervously, but I grabbed his hand. "Let's go," I said, and we crossed the threshold.

We were lucky. Or led inside, maybe, by some unseen hand toward safety. My nonna's ghost over my shoulder, whispering, *I always wanted you to see this.* I was on a journey toward her, after all. Visiting the region where she was born, a few years after her death, despite my empty bank account and absent job prospects. I had never been to Italy before, but I felt like we crossed through a gate of memory as we entered Pompeii. At that gate, I thought of Ariadne, the goddess of the labyrinth, and her magical spool of red string: the string she gave to Theseus to help him safely return. We had no red string; no tourist map of the grounds even. But unlike Theseus, it was unlikely we would encounter a minotaur in the labyrinth's centre, so we went ahead.

The ancient streets led between broken walls and arches. The sky was grey and I kept glancing up at the silhouette of Vesuvius looming above us, mostly hidden in cloud. I was waiting for the moment it would reveal itself—a giant tower of black rock that had laid this place bare. There are two fault lines running through Italy, two boundary lines where the tectonic plates meet—one from the north to the south, another from the east to the west. They cross each other not far from Pompeii and form a rare, natural X on the tectonic map of the world. They also make Italy one of the most earthquake-prone places on earth. If Pompeii is a monument, it is a monument to these tectonics: a museum of the earth's sudden and staggering power. But of course, it is also a graveyard. And it's the deaths that draw many people to its gates.

School groups and tourists rushed ahead of us, all in the same direction. They were going, we figured, where the maps we didn't have told them to go. But we turned the other way. It felt good to walk apart from the crowds, without destination, observing the once-destroyed world around us. We turned down the quietest streets we could, hands interwoven, and studied painted frescos on stone walls. It was hard to tell what was original and what was a reconstruction. I began to play a game of *Real or Fake* in my mind, and kept getting the answer wrong. *Real, real, real*, was the truth.

Or, at other times: both. The world around us was more a collaboration than a replica. The earth had shaken down those arches, buried them in pyroclastic flow, and millennia later people had lifted them back up. Where mending was needed, they mended.

If I'd crossed through a gate of memory, I'd also crossed through a gate of time. And it wasn't just the past I'd entered, but the meeting place of past, present, and future. This is the constant work in Pompeii: unearthing, reconstructing, preserving for generations to come. The ruins are perhaps the best-preserved disaster in the world. And the longer we study them, the deeper we dig into them, the more we discover how death looks when it meets the sudden hand of disaster.

Eventually, we got caught up in a stream of people. There was no easy way through the crowd. Under the hazy, grey sky, I could blur my eyes to the past and see it: groups of us running through the streets, toward the idea of safety. How much warning would we have if the volcano decided to erupt? What would we do if an earthquake started? All around us were broken things, half-fallen walls ready to collapse again. It was easy to see how a stampede could begin. Did I even know the path back to the entrance? No. Maybe if I had a tourist map, I'd have been safer. Or, say, a spool of Ariadne's magical thread.

"Are you okay?" My partner asked me gently, placing a hand on my back. I closed my eyes, and blinked myself back to the present. "It's just a lot of people," I responded, as if we weren't standing in a famous monument to threat. As if Vesuvius didn't make me nervous. And just then, the volcano revealed itself. Between two clouds, I finally saw it: enormous and capped with snow. "Look," I said, as we stood together in the sudden sunlight.

"It's so close," he said, and I nodded. I could feel its closeness, its staggering presence, like my hand was moving close to an oven. It was hard not to wonder about those who lived in Pompeii—the choice to reside at the edge of a force like that, with the possibility of eruption. But that's not how they lived, I've discovered. The volcano hadn't erupted in over a thousand years; the citizens of Pompeii only knew about earthquakes, and that's what they felt: earthquake upon earthquake, growing steadily worse.

Clouds covered the summit, and we went forward alongside the crowd. That's the thing about curiosity; it gets difficult to turn away from a shared destination. Ahead of us, people were crowded around a display case, laughing. Neither of us knew what was inside until a spot cleared for us to get closer. And then we saw it: a man lying there frozen, one hand reaching toward the sky—toward the heavens, toward the glass where we stood above him. It looked like he was covered in stone; sealed in a sarcophagus of the ash that fell during the eruption of Pompeii. *Real or fake?* The question flipped in my mind like a coin toss: *real*—it had to be. The terror on his face; the trill of the crowd. I reached my hand toward his, as if we could touch through the glass, through the disaster, through almost two thousand years. Around me, the crowd continued laughing. I felt a twisting sense of deep discomfort: *Is this how we should honour the dead?*

"It doesn't seem right," I muttered. "Those are bodies." My partner shook his head in wonder, and we stepped away from the glass. There were figures all through the courtyard; I could see that now. As if we'd reached the centre of the labyrinth, and a minotaur lived there after all.

MANY PEOPLE SEE those figures as I did, as victims turned to stone by the volcano. But I was wrong when I flipped my coin:

real or fake? I imagined mummified remains within the stone, like insects trapped in amber. But they are not bodies, exactly. Instead, they are plaster castings of the people who lived here—those who could not escape—captured at the moment of their death. When Vesuvius erupted in 79 AD, it sent forth an enormous cloud of ash, smoke, and volcanic glass. Recently, it's been suggested it took only fifteen minutes for this pyroclastic plume to kill those who remained. Everything was frozen in place in Pompeii, sunk under metres of ash and preserved. The bodies wore away within the stone, but they left a perfect imprint. In the mid-1800s, archeologist Giuseppe Fiorelli conceived to pour a form of liquid plaster into the cavities where they had started to discover remains—the same way sculptures are cast. And from the negative space in the stone, the *Plaster Citizens* arose.

The *Plaster Citizens of Pompeii*, as they are called, tell the clearest story of what happened: hands clenched, dresses askew. There is only one eyewitness account of the eruption, and it is the oldest volcanologist report on record. From the Bay of Naples, on the outer circles of the eruption's impact, Pliny the Younger watched as his village, Misenum, turn grey. "I looked round," he writes. "A dense black cloud was coming up behind us, spreading over the earth like a flood … darkness fell, not the dark of a moonless or cloudy night, but as if the lamp had been put out in a closed room."

It is estimated twenty thousand Romans lived in Pompeii, but only two thousand are thought to have died there. It's believed most of these people were servants, or facing enslavement, and it's unlikely they were given a choice or opportunity to flee. Some wealthy Romans remained, as well—averting their minds, maybe, from the ever-growing quakes, protecting their possessions from the looting they worried would follow. Looting did follow—and follows still: objects are constantly taken from the site of Pompeii. Some of great value, which are then sold in underground markets. Others, like pebbles and tiles, are often taken as mementos. But every year, hundreds of these keepsakes are sent back to Pompeii with apologies, from tourists who feel they have been haunted—struck with bad luck for years—since taking objects from the excavated grounds.

My ancestors would not have been surprised by this. Who steals from a gravesite, and expects to sleep soundly? Because of Pliny's records, it was long believed the eruption began in August, within twenty-four hours of *Vulcanalia*, the annual Roman holy day dedicated to the god of fire. But recently, the timeline of the explosion has been updated, due to a piece of ancient graffiti. It's now thought Vesuvius erupted in late October—a few days from what became known as *i Morti* in Italy, *il Giorno dei Morti*, or Day of the Dead—a time when the veil between the living and the dead is said to be thin, and spirits often visit.

STANDING IN THAT courtyard, that veil felt thin—even in May. We were standing, I know now, in the Garden of the Fugitives, where thirteen figures were found. They have been left as they were, positioned exactly where archeologists found them. The orchard, a singular kind of graveyard. Maybe it is right and good to laugh and run through the ruins, around the display of those bodies. Children bringing life back to what was buried, then broken back open and excavated. With perspective, I can see that joy is necessary, like kids skipping through a cemetery on *i Morti*, plucking white flowers from the grass. There are many ways to honour the dead, to unmake a haunting, and I know only a few of those ways. But the bodies in Pompeii are not headstones, or pieces of art. They are not symbols. They are casts of people caught with their mouths open, taken by the sudden hand of nature. Through the gates, the threat felt both ancient and imminent. Past, written in stone—but also present, frozen midsentence, reaching for another breath. We stood on the flank of that same active volcano, staring at those figures, and it was like my hand could touch the plaster hands in the case. What was glass, what was two thousand years, between us?

We walked for many hours that day, until we were thirsty and tired. In the photographs, I look stoic under the grey sky. We sat on the replica of a ruin and ate plums. We kept our eyes on the looming figure of the volcano above us. The volcano is quiet, but not dormant; it has erupted thirty times since Pompeii. Vesuvius sits atop a 1,400-square-kilometre layer of magma; another eruption is inevitable. For all of our science, we still cannot say if this threat is imminent or distant. Over three million people now live in the area surrounding the volcano—over six hundred thousand directly in the red zone—making it the most densely populated volcanic region in the world.

These numbers echo. The glass of the display case disappears. Eventually, all our hands may touch the hands of the plaster citizens, frozen in time. Recognition of a threat does not change our proximity to that threat; denial does not make it go away. The truth is, the evacuation plan for Vesuvius is mostly based on the eruption patterns of 1631 and has been widely criticized.[1] Volcanology can only offer warnings, not predictions. When the time comes, it is unlikely anyone will be properly prepared.

It is redundant to ask why Pompeiians lived here, when we've come back and settled around it, used it as an amusement park. They didn't know about the eruptions in 79 AD—but we do. So we must believe that the crisis will not happen *now*; that it will not happen to *us*. We must believe that there will be enough foresight, sufficient and effective warnings, that we will be *saved*. How else could we stand on these ruins, live in this shadow?

The last eruption of Vesuvius took place in 1944, just before my grandmother left southern Italy to come to Canada. Thirty-six people died from the ash. I thought of her as we finally looked for an exit. I pictured her listening to the news reports on an old radio, with her sisters. She grew up on the north-south fault, in mountains that rose from the clashing of the plates. Her relatives had lost their homes—entire villages had collapsed, due to quakes. I tried to imagine the expression on their faces as the earth shook beneath them that day. Did they climb into the cellar and pray? Or just tend to the caged rabbits in the yard, knowing the mountain would choose its own future, like mountains always do.

The streets turned and turned as we wandered; it was difficult to find our way. But finally I saw—not a red string—but a red arrow on a sign pointing toward the exit of Pompeii. If not Ariadne, then my grandmother beside me, whispering: *This way.*

MOUNTAIN THAT EATS MEN

Cerro Rico, Potosí, Bolivia

THE DARKNESS DEEPENS as I enter a shaft in the earth. It is a rock tunnel so narrow I have to get down on my hands and knees. I crawl into the dark—my helmet and headlamp shifting, moving light—until I emerge in an antechamber of the mountain, where candles and lanterns are lit. Men are laughing around me; American men, smiling, their blond hair showing from beneath their helmets. There are coca leaves in my teeth: rich and bitter, numbing my tongue and gums. I'm out of breath already; there isn't much oxygen at this altitude, and even less underground. Deep in the mountain, everything is compressed: the air, the veins of metal, the history running between and beneath us.

I am standing in La Negra mine in Cerro Rico—"Rich Hill," the Spanish called it. Mostly, it is known by a different name now: *the mountain that eats men*. Eight million people are said to have died here. Standing in the antechamber, the men's laughter echoes, and I don't know that yet; I don't know the depth of the mine, the depth of the loss, or the name it carries.

"Estás bien?" our guide, Miguel asks me. I'm still breathing heavily. He tells me to chew more of the coca leaves, and I do. They are a mild stimulant in this form, used as medicine to help with altitude. Then he hands me back what I bought at the market above—tobacco, coca leaves, and corn liquor—to offer to the god of this place. *El Tío*, uncle, the devil. In the centre of the room, El Tío sits adorned with cigarettes and flowers, small bottles of eighty-proof. The figure is life-size and umber red, like ore and iron, or how blood might look in this place. Two horns on his head, garlands around his neck: he is made of clay and plaster— made of the mountain itself, maybe. He stares at me, at the wall of the chamber, like he is looking through time. The men pose by him for photographs, each flashing a different posture, always smiling. I didn't bring a camera with me. Instead, I bend down by the statue. Place the liquor at El Tío's feet, like Miguel told me to, then some cigarettes and the paper bag of leaves.

If the mines of the world went deep enough, there could be a place in the darkness where they all meet. A fault line where the gold of the tunnels beneath northern Ontario, where my mother was born, meet the last of the silver hidden here. That's what I think, discordantly, when I kneel at Tío's feet: *This could be home. This could lead home.* I think, as well, of the gold thirteen on my nonna's necklace, and the tarot cards I was given by my father when I turned thirteen. On one card: the image of the devil.

Placed on my alter, by flowers, lit candles. I was taught to read the card as a reflection of power. The power within us, the power beyond us. In the flickering light, bent at Tío's feet, I find stillness in me, prayerlike quiet. I close my eyes for a second, whisper a word for the safety of the miners. Then dynamite is blasted below us, and the very ground shakes.

"Are you ready?" Miguel asks, as I rise from my knees. "Now we'll go into the mine."

•

ON THEIR OWN, mountains simply stand against the sky: enormous, ancient, tectonic. They will eat men with earthquakes, with eruptions—like Vesuvius did to the citizens of Pompeii—but that's not how Cerro Rico got its name. In 1545, Spanish colonialists found out about the large deposits of silver in the mountain, and it became the global epicentre of their extractive colonial project. In Eduardo Galeano's seminal book *Open Veins of Latin America*, he painted the scale of their violence: "You could build a silver bridge from Potosí to Madrid from what was mined here—and one back with the bones of those that died taking it out."

This violence goes to the foundation of our contemporary world. The silver extracted from Cerro Rico became a core source of wealth for the Spanish Empire, and was used to fund their wars against the British, French, and Dutch, as well as the Ottoman Empire, transforming the economic and political landscape of the world. As a result, Potosí has been called the "first city of capitalism." Cerro Rico has also been cited as the source of the first global currency: Spanish "pieces of eight." Many believe the dollar sign originated from these silver coins, which were stamped with the mark of the Potosí mine in the form of overlapping letters: *PTSI—$*.[1] In 1776, Adam Smith also wrote about the silver trade that grew from Potosí in *The Wealth of Nations*, a work largely cited as the foundational text for free-market capitalism. So beyond the silver that was taken from Cerro Rico, a narrative was extracted—and that narrative shapes the economy of our world.

•

IN THE SHADOWS in La Negra mine, I can feel the weight and enormous size of my borrowed coveralls. My helmet slides all over my head, no matter how much I tighten the strap. I know it's not safe to go forward, but I do. I want to know, want to see what's beneath us.

At the passageway of the next descent, a metal ladder peeks up from the hole. "I'll go first," Miguel says, smiling, and then he is quickly eaten by the dark.

"Can I go next?" I ask the men beside me, because I know I'll lose my nerve if I wait. They nod, and I tighten the useless strap of my helmet, wishing the headlamp were steadier, brighter. I look one last time at the figure in the centre of the room, in the flickering candlelight. Then I descend on the shaking ladder into El Tío's domain, into *the mountain that eats men*, into darkness.

•

I DID NOT go to Cerro Rico to report on the journey. I didn't plan to go there at all. I was travelling alone in Bolivia before heading to a symposium of artists from across the Americas, to present my work in Buenos Aires. That day in Potosí, I walked through the town in the rain. I went to the mine because it was a day of celebration. It was 2007, and there were hundreds of llamas tied together in small herds in the streets. They were waiting to be sacrificed, I was told, and there were extra that year in thanks for good profits: strong veins of minerals had been found. Evo Morales had come into power a year before—a former *cocalero* (coca leaf grower), and the first Indigenous president of Bolivia— and his platform had been designed to give hope to the people of Potosí.[2] He was in the midst of nationalizing the country's oil and gas sector, and there was widespread hope this would improve the quality of life for many people.

While I knew little of the Cerro, I knew about the election of Morales, and something about resource control in Bolivia. Specifically, I knew that the government had once privatized the rain. In 1999, the president of Bolivia—Hugo Banzer, a former dictator—agreed to privatize the nation's remaining public enterprises, including water services, as a requirement of a loan of $138 million from the International Monetary Fund. Under this privatization, it became illegal to collect water for personal use— for drinking, bathing, growing food—without a permit from the corporation (American-owned Bechtel, via subsidiaries). Simultaneously, water bills doubled and tripled in communities already facing systematic impoverishment, with some of the lowest per capita incomes in the world. Widespread protests broke out in 2000, in defence of water rights. A violent government response followed, resulting in multiple deaths. These events are known as the Cochabamba Water Crisis, the Water Revolt, or the Water War, and they speak to the continued level of foreign interest in resource control in Bolivia: even rain water came into view of the international market.[3]

There was dynamite being blasted like fireworks as I climbed those streets that day. The rain grew stronger, and I remember thinking about Cochabamba, about what the president of the World Bank famously said in 2000, in response to the Water War: "The biggest problem with water, is the waste of water through lack of charging."[4] I was sixteen when he said that. I was tear-gassed in Quebec City that year, protesting the World Bank and the Free Trade Area of the Americas. And nearly a decade later, I still had so much more to learn. Bolivia has endured more coup d'états than any other nation in the world—nearly two hundred since the official declaration of independence in 1825. And these coups, as well as the Water War, all seem to rise from the mountain; from the legacy of resource extraction and foreign intervention that began with the Spanish, and seems to have no end. (For more on this, see The Understory: "On The Lithium Coup," page 219.)

I arrived at the market that surrounded the mines, thinking about water—and thinking, too, about where I was headed in Argentina: an *encuentro* of hundreds of artists, gathering to discuss *cuerpoliticas*—body politics. Where the body meets public policy, the market; where the body meets violence and resistance—and where it meets art. In the market by the mines, I met Miguel. He told me about the cooperatives that operate inside the mines, and I joined his tour. I wanted to understand more. Not as a journalist or an artist, even—more as a young person trying to have a conversation with life. It's like that for many of us, I think: we want to have a conversation with life, and we enter the story without knowing its end. We enter the story, we go into the mountain, without understanding our place in it. Without knowing the harm, the risk, or the cost.

·

WHAT DO I see in the centre of the mountain?

Nothing. I climb down the ladder, I descend into the mountain, and everything is dark. No vision, no memory exists for me there. This is not a metaphor or a symbol: in the heart of the mountain, I see absolutely nothing. I can't remember what happens there. There is a blank mark in my mind, as if I've shut my eyes, reached the threshold of my oxygen, of my tolerance, and the mountain eats the memory up.

•

A SINKHOLE OPENED at the peak of Cerro Rico in 2011. Since then, it has continued to widen. "Total collapse is possible," engineer Nestor Rene Espinoza reported, after completing comprehensive studies on the mountain. "We hope that this does not happen in Cerro Rico."[5]

With each year, the mountain loses more cohesion, fewer deposits of tin, minerals, and ore can be found—let alone silver—and the risk to miners increases. Despite this instability, it is unlikely mining in the Cerro—even in the highest-risk areas—will end. Numerous decrees have been passed to both limit and suspend mining in the high-risk areas of mountain, to prevent the collapse of Cerro Rico, and the city of Potosí that surrounds it. But there are a tangle of relationships that lead to its continuation—and many of them are difficult to see; they flicker to light, like my half-broken headlamp in the mine, and then disappear into the shadow of foreign-owned subsidiaries again. In 2014, the Morales government discovered that more than forty cooperatives held joint contracts with multinational corporations and their subsidiaries, and these corporations were operating at enormous extranational profits, while exerting substantial political pressure on local officials. Unsurprisingly, these extranational profits have not translated into any improvement to the income or quality of life for the majority of miners.[6]

When I met Miguel in the market, it sounded like worker's rights might be front and centre in the cooperatives, with profits shared locally between miners. But I took that mostly from the echoes of the word, and from what I knew of cooperatives back home. In reality, it is estimated that conditions have barely improved in hundreds of years. While official cooperative and unionized miners can receive a relatively good income, depending on the veins of minerals they find, the vast majority of people working in the mines do so as day labourers, with no protection for their rights, health or wages. The unregulated rates are often as low as $3–$5 a day, and many of these miners begin work when they are still children. UNICEF has stated that 10 percent of miners in Bolivia may be children. MUSOL, a women's collective from Potosí, reports that approximately fourteen women who are married to cooperative miners are widowed each month. This is likely a modest estimate, because it only reflects members of the cooperatives and does not include those who die as a result of the health hazards of mining, specifically silicosis of the lungs.[7]

This is the world I climbed into, not knowing where I stood: pathways of extraction that run through more than one hundred kilometres, across six hundred mines and five hundred years. The Bolivian government has attempted to stabilize the summit with ultralight cement since 2011, but the sinkhole has continued to widen. How could it not? Spain is said to have extracted 1.4 billion ounces of silver from the mountain, and that extraction has carried on. It is estimated the number of miners in Cerro Rico has doubled since I was there in 2007. What choice are families left with, in a context of ongoing hunger? In a context where the discourse of "trickle-down economics" once resulted in the privatization of the rain?

FIFTEEN YEARS SINCE my visit: survival mining has grown, and survival tourism as well. In a context of limited options, one option is to build an economy of witness—a business model where we shadow the miners into the shadows of the mountain. When I picture the scene around El Tío now, it's not lit by candles. It's lit by the flash of a dozen iPhones, over and over. And the laughter of the crowd expands, their laughter goes on—someone points to the figure's clay phallus, someone poses beside it. When you research the conditions faced by the miners, you also find ads for tours. "How to Take a Tour of Bolivia's Most Deadly Mine," one reads. The words are set against a photograph of a bright blue sky. *How to* climb inside the possible collapse, they mean; *how to* place a hand on the missing vein of silver; *how to* watch poverty touch lives in Cerro Rico.

My tour guide worked for Green-Go Tours, one of the first companies to be established in Potosí. It was created by former miner Julio Morales. But Morales shut his company down in 2019. "They don't care about the miners," he said in a recent interview, referring to the tourists, "they just want selfies." Four of his friends had recently died in an accident in the mines, when he was interviewed. "They are going to a real mine, where miners die," he added.[8]

Everything taken from the mountain has a cost, be it silver or selfie or story. I climbed right into the rung of this industry, to the feet of El Tío and beyond. I entered that same economy of witness. So maybe this is what I cannot recall at the bottom of the ladder: a mirror. My own face glowing back at me, the reflection asking: *What the hell are you doing down here?* Because good intentions will never erase the complexities of power—in mining, in tourism, or beyond.

I hear Julio Morales' words, over and over. I retrace my steps and look for an answer in the dark. A week after I visited the mines, I arrived at the *encuentro* in Buenos Aires and began an intensive with renowned Mexican/Chicano performance artist Guillermo Gómez-Peña of La Pocha Nostra. The first thing he asked us to do, the first morning, was close our eyes and run.

What is your relationship to control? the devil card asks; the practice of Gómez-Peña asks. And the descent into the mountain reckons with your answer.

SOUTH OF CERRO Rico lies Salar de Uyuni, the world's largest natural mirror. It is over ten thousand square kilometres, a salt flat created by a prehistoric lake that disappeared. In rainy season, when water collects here, it forms a reflective surface so enormous it can be seen from space. The sky reflects on the earth and creates optical illusions. There is no horizon line in sight, and often no indication where sky and earth split; people go there to take photographs that mess with perspective and scale. They stand on the sky; they walk through starry heavens. It is said to be one of the most beautiful places on earth. And it is also home to more than half of the world's lithium.

What silver was to currency, lithium could be to renewable energy. It is a key, strategic resource used to create power sources, from phone batteries to electric cars and solar panels. The more we turn to hybrid and electric vehicles; the more our technology becomes portable, and our homes off-grid, the more demand there is for lithium. But lithium itself is not renewable. It is a finite mineral, mostly located in one of the driest places on earth, and its extraction requires enormous amounts of water. Already, where lithium extraction has begun in Chile's nearby Salar de Atacama, it has sucked dry over 60 percent of available water in the region.[9]

The Salar de Uyuni resides in the shadow of the Cerro—they share an environmental context and political history, if not a future. In November 2019, in the midst of widespread protests, Evo Morales was compelled to resign by the police and military of Bolivia. This event is sometimes called the *lithium coup*, and Morales and his party maintain it took place over control of lithium resources, just as previous coups were seen to be related to resource control.[10] The international community remains divided about whether this is true, and what exactly took place. But one thing is clearly documented: in response to public concerns that the erosion of democracy in Bolivia was connected to renewable energy sources, Elon Musk tweeted: "We coup who we want, deal with it!"[11]

Musk's joke is the same joke being made in the antechamber, I think. I look back to the chamber: I try to get my bearings; American men laugh around me. Is it funny? To see power carved out like that—in a tweet, or in a sculpture, in an underground den? Does it matter if Musk meant Bolivia in 2019, or elsewhere? America has backed a legacy of coups, so his tweet is honest, at least. The way dynamite is honest, the way stone is honest in a rockfall. Maybe the truths we face are funny, maybe they're uncomfortable, so we laugh; maybe we need to black them out. Maybe there are a hundred ways to turn from what we witness, and still: this story ends up on the largest mirror on earth. Standing on the lithium flats, you see yourself wherever you go.

Take a photo of the ground: it's a selfie.

SILVER DWINDLES IN Cerro Rico; the summit loses cohesion. But instead of foreign interests turning away, they turn toward it. Not just for the lithium south of the mountain; new silver-extraction projects are being established in the areas surrounding Potosí. In the midst of widespread uncertainty about the state of democracy in Bolivia, speculation about its economic future rapidly shifted as "silver sands" projects were established. These are open pit mines that depend on sifting through large areas for sediment and smaller grains to process, including the mining offshoots left behind by the Spanish conquistadors' legacy of enslavement and extraction.

Is this what we call *sustainability*? Shifting through the physical remains of history. More dust, more sediment, as the mountain collapses. What is *sustained*, then? Like the extraction of lithium, this process requires enormous amounts of water, in an area where Indigenous farmers are already often unable to maintain their crops due to drought. And so the farmers are brought to the mines, to the mountain, as the mountain falls in: *dust to dust.* And we follow underground, shadows of a shadow, taking photographs, with lithium batteries in our phones.

What would allow this to end—the survival mining, and the tourism of survival? You can't un-mine a mountain. You can't return the silver taken from the dark, or repair the eroded veins of tin and ore. Who should pay for the summit of Cerro Rico to be stabilized? The World Bank offers loans for the repairs and economic growth, with contingencies the rain remembers. Spain averts its eyes. The silver they extracted translates to close to $40 billion, before interest. "We coup who we want," Musk types, turning up the volume on nineties grunge. LOL, the internet responds. The day after Morales was removed from power, Tesla's stocks rose substantially, and they have continued to rise since. Capitalism rose from violence in Potosí, and the story Adam Smith told about it. *Look,* Smith basically tweeted, *look what happened with the silver in Potosí,* and then he suggested we should trust the invisible hand of capitalism; we should just let it be. But there is a visible hand in the history of the mountain. There is a force that eats men, and it is not nature, it's not only chaos.

IN THE SUMMER of 2020, the *Financial Post* published an article titled "The Imperial City Is Reborn."[12] It made no reference to the lives lost due to imperialism in Cerro Rico, or the worker-led revolutions that followed. Instead, it split Galeano's famous quote in half: "You could build a bridge of pure silver from Potosí to Madrid with the amount of ore extracted," the article simply read.

In this rebrand, a quote illustrating the violence of the imperial project became a quote used to illustrate imperialism's success. What would this mean to Eduardo Galeano? Galeano famously said: "I'm a writer ... obsessed with remembering, obsessed with remembering the past of America, and above all that of Latin America, intimate land condemned to amnesia."[13]

It matters, then, to remember—to know the second half of Galeano's quote, and that his words are not a metaphor; they are a measure. The silver does not exist without extraction, and extraction has a bottomless cost: eight million lives, in a single mountain.

Is this the city that the article suggests will be reborn? Like Galeano, we may all be called to become "obsessed with remembering." If not obsessed, then concerned—committed—to remembering this history despite the inertia that pulls against it, saying *forget, forget.* Where the sentence itself is being erased, deleted word by word, it bears repeating again: "You could build a silver bridge from Potosí to Madrid from what was mined here," Galeano wrote, "and one back with the bones of those that died taking it out."

FOR A MOUNTAIN to form, tectonic plates have to clash together and raise stone from the very centre of the earth. And it's like that; it's like we've clashed the plates beneath Potosí again and again, to raise a world economy. Cerro Rico is not a theory. The miners are not a symbol. But PTSI, the dollar sign stamped on the silver—that is a symbol. It's perhaps *the* symbol, the strongest shared metaphor between us. It shapes all our lives. We touch it and we touch the ancient silicosis: the first dust rising in the first miner's lungs. Our world is built in the shadow of this mountain, and this mountain—quite literally—is ready to fall in.

I understood little about the depths of where I stood, that day in Potosí. But I was right when I knelt at the feet of El Tío: there is a place in Cerro Rico where all mines meet. This is not a metaphor; it is a fact written on the NASDAQ, on the DOW, on every dollar bill: PTSI, $. This history belongs to us all, and you don't need to enter the mountain to touch it.

One of the meanings of the devil tarot card is *binding.* That we are bound, sometimes chained, to systems and patterns of the world and its history. Pretending they are absent does not make them disappear. Liberation and power: these are questions of relationship, interconnection. My devil, my tarot card—the *horned god,* he is sometimes called—that's not who lives in Cerro Rico. But maybe they are something like cousins—if only connected through the church that tried to make them disappear, and instead created hybrids. Both, perhaps, reminders that the ground beneath our feet is alive and sacred, and that its power is ultimately beyond our control.

Tío, *uncle,* the devil in Potosí: his rituals are said to have arisen from Indigenous cosmology of the mountains mixed with Spanish Catholicism, and also as a form of resistance to exploitation by colonial powers. In *We Eat the Mines and the Mines Eat Us,* author June Nash points to how the practice of making offerings to El Tío—*ch'alla*—were crucial in creating solidarity among miners: "That solidarity, cemented in the cult of the gods of the underworld, created the strongest platform from which to resist, and successfully reject, the demands of the so-called tin barons."[14]

Liberation and power; relationship and interconnection. We are part of what is: the earth, the extraction, and the story in its wake. It is a story of resistance and faith, as well as exploitation. And it is a story that is still being written. Despite what the church says, what the Spanish might declare, or the World Bank: the mountain will choose its own future, in the end. The mountain belongs to itself.

·

WHAT DO I see in the centre of the mountain?

I peer into my memory of the *nothing,* and the nothing is there. Just the dark, and more darkness. I reach the bottom rung of the shaking ladder—I remember that part, the unstable ladder beneath me—and then my mind takes from me what I cannot handle. Or maybe—this is what I wonder now—maybe deep in that mountain, I touch a vein where all worlds meet. Where the silver of Potosí becomes the gold of Northern Ontario, where the drills go so deep you can feel the heat seep around you. That silver, that gold: it is the world touching itself, over and over. It is where our lives collide: in currency, in history, in symbol. And maybe my mind can't make sense of it; my body can't hold it—this collision of heat and history, this *inferno*, the sun at the centre of our lives—and so I blank. The headlight turns off in my mind. I am alone in the dark, and El Tío echoes: his statue comes to me over and over; that's all I can see.

That's all I see until I climb the half-broken ladder, back up to the chamber where he resides. I can hear explosions in the distance, both below and above me. They are shattering open another vein of the mine in the darkness. They are lighting dynamite like fireworks in the daylight above. "*Vamos,*" our guide says—he's the last up the ladder. *Let's go.* There's soot on his face now, on all of our faces, in our mouths and eyes. He leads us along the tunnel, returning the way that we've come. I crouch down on all fours again, at the mouth of the narrow tunnel. I slide my way through, back up to the light. And there it is: the light, the daylight. The mountain hasn't fallen upon us. We've risen back to our lives.

BLOOD STONES:
AN INVENTORY

THERE WAS A store in Toronto that used to be my favourite place to grieve. When I couldn't hold on to the sadness I was carrying any longer, I would go there and hold on to stones. The store was filled with them: clear crystals, black pebbles, and jasper bloodstone. Some rocks were the size of a hand, or a heart. Others were bigger, and they sat on the floor: open geodes of purple amethyst that reached up to your thigh. In the back corner, the cheapest stones were piled into bowls. Those were the ones I went for: rough-cut ounces of jasper, chrysocolla, pyrite, citrine, and malachite. You could touch them all before you decided what to buy, and I would palm them. I'd wait until my hands got warm or heavy, and listen for the smallest voice inside me to nudge me from one cut to the other. Then I'd hold that rock to my skin, to the light, and ask the silence if we were meant to be together.

It was good to grieve like that, to place what I'd lost—my boy-friend, my girlfriend, my job, my joy—in stone and notice the colour, see how it changed when sun ran through it. The small rocks were always less than ten dollars; only more if you wanted them set in jewellery, which I couldn't afford, just like I couldn't afford therapy to deal with my grief. The waiting list to see a counsellor at Planned Parenthood was two years long, and I was only halfway through it. That store, those five-dollar rocks: they were how I was trying to get by. It was like that for most of my friends. The day one friend's father died and she just wanted to drink beers on a patio; we did what we'd learned to do with our poverty and depression: we bought onyx and turquoise instead of flowers. We ate french fries with her as she clutched those crystals, and made her drink water so she didn't get too drunk before dusk.

The work of survival is never simple. We do the best we can with our grief. It's not that I've stopped believing these acts have a purpose; it's that now I think of the miner, the mine, and the extraction, and what I find in the stone is no longer relief.

A DECADE HAS passed since I loitered in that store, crying behind my sunglasses over chips of rose quartz. The store shut down, but not because it went bankrupt. It moved into a building six times the size; a corner lot with two stories, large windows, and a reiki studio upstairs. The store expanded the way the crystal trade has, booming over the last decade to become a multi-billion-dollar industry. In the first wave of the pandemic, head-lines about crystals kept showing up: "The Market for Crystals Is Outshining Diamonds in the Covid Era;" "American Anxiety Drives a Crystal Boom." But there were other headlines, as well. *The Guardian* published an article titled: "Are Crystals the New Blood Diamonds?" And the answer appears to be yes. *The Guardian* cites Global Witness, an international mining watchdog, that found the Taliban earns up to twenty million dollars a year from Afghanistan's lapis lazuli mines, and quotes Payal Sampat of the nonprofit Earthworks: "It is impossible to know for sure," Sampat says, "if your crystal was obtained via an environmental and human rights horror show."[1]

There is no governing body for the extraction and trade of "healing" crystals. There are no international regulations regarding labour and environmental practices. There are no set principles for what constitutes *ethical* sourcing. To trace a stone to its mountain may only be possible for a person who studies the atomic structure of gems; someone who can match minerals to their source, through a database of the world's terra forma. Even then, it can take a geologist, an economist, and a political scientist, and sometimes a journalist, alongside the willingness of both corporations and the state, to trace the full movement of a rock to a hand. The truth is: most of these crystals are by-products of mines focused on the extraction of other minerals and stones.[2] So we may be praying to a gold or titanium mine; we may be holding a stone that blood was spilled on, a rock shattered by machines and dynamite, and muttering: *Oh moonlight—Oh goddess—protect the earth.*

Headlines are headlines; language is not the same as a life. I try to remember that. There is a miner, right now, climbing down a mine to break open a vein of tourmaline. And it's that miner's body, their name and growing silicosis, that I'm trying to see through the refraction of language. It's their hand I touch when I touch the stones.

Quartz

A hard, crystalline mineral composed of silicon and oxygen. Second-most common mineral in the Earth's crust. Known for alignment and amplification. Sometimes called the stone of power.

BENEATH EACH STONE in the crystal store was a slip of paper that listed its energetic properties: *grounding, protection, clarity.* You could take those papers with you so you wouldn't forget how to work with them when you got home. Only some of those papers listed where the stone had been extracted from: Tibet, South Africa. Some of the crystals were listed as coming from Brazil, I remember, because I was drawn to them more than others. As if touching the piece of quartz could connect me back to the cliff in Chapada dos Guimãraes, where I stood at eighteen, watching butterflies soar above a thousand-foot drop, the canyon wide open and green. There was natural quartz all over that place: unmined, uncut, just existing there by your feet, small stones of it on every path. The dream was—the dream naturally is, I think, if we aren't vigilant—that many stones are simply picked up, gathered, and sent to us; that there's no violence or harm involved. That you could have found the stone, just as easily, if you stood on the mountain yourself.

The places where we touch—each other and the world—is this part of the draw? We touch a fragment, a piece of the *elsewhere*— and it brings us there. There is an intimacy in the act, there has to be: between the hand and the stone, atoms change place; the ore rubs gently into the skin.

The elsewhere and the intangible; they're both in the stone— and I've heard both of them call to me. For years, I carried a piece of quartz hanging from a pendant above my heart, until it broke in two while I sat in still meditation. I opened my eyes and there it was in my lap, in shards. It's not that I have stopped believing in things I can't understand; I believe in the unknown and that it is powerful beyond measure. But for a long time I thought these were mainly questions of worship.

I bought my quartz necklace on Salt Spring Island, from a woman who sold rocks at the farmers' market. She worked under a white tent and always wore white dresses. It was 2010; the same summer I was bitten by a tick. I was living on the farm, volunteering in the kitchen, and I wanted to bring a piece of the island home with me. The woman said the stone was from Salt Spring, and I believed her in a meaningful way. There's quartz all over the island; it's in the bedrock of the island itself. The mountains and cliffs have veins of it, and you can find crystals when you hike. You can run your hand over the sharp edge, where it is still part of a boulder. You can pick up a loose stone, opaque and milky, tinted pink. Though, it matters to ask: should you do that? If you're like me, an uninvited visitor on occupied lands, should you pick up loose, sovereign stones on a mountain, and say *beautiful*, or *blessed*, or *mine*?

The pendant she sold me looked nothing like what I saw in the woods. It was clear and cut into a hexagon. I watched her shape the wire around the stone just for me, and it felt precious. It is possible that the quartz was locally gathered. If so, it was likely from so-called Mount Maxwell—traditionally known as Hwmet'atsum (Bent Over Place), an important sacred site of the Quw'utsun (Cowichan) Nation.[3] Perhaps that woman had received permission to gather and sell the quartz. But more likely, the crystal did not come from Salt Spring at all, and was brought to the island from a foreign mine, where it could be extracted and cut into its hexagon shape for less than the cost of a locally grown flower.

I know it's not always like this: extraction for profit, worship as currency, as colonial act. There are traditional practices with stones and crystals all over the world, found on every continent; varied cultural and spiritual relationships that guide communities forward with integrity—in the uses of the stone, in the methods of gathering them. Even in ancient Pompeii, a priestess's case was recently found in the ash, and in it were crystals and stones. I think of my grandmother and her lucky rabbit's foot—she tended and killed those rabbits herself. They lived well, and died well, and every part of them was used. We are part of what we worship, the memory teaches me, and there are rightful practices for each of us. When we touch the object, we touch our faith, we touch our bloodline, and we touch the object's production—how it came to be in our hands: through generosity and lineage, or maybe industry and theft. And unfortunately, what we find in a rock store, at a market stand, on Etsy, is mostly the latter.

Power, amplification, alignment with the unknown. If these are the promises of the quartz, then they are fulfilled by the market, by the trade, by the pathways of currency and extraction that echo and echo, without ever letting themselves be seen.

Rhodochrocite

A manganese carbonate ore. From the Greek "rhodes" (pink) and "khros" (colour). Most often sourced in silver mines. Known as a stone of compassion, healing, and unconditional love.

RHODOCHROSITE IS BEAUTIFUL. It's pink and marked with small black circles and veins, like a heart. It's a stone for love, for healing what life does to everyone, at some point: leaving us in the back alley of a relationship we thought would go on forever, where someone has spray-painted illegible words, and no one has cleaned up the dead leaves for years. In the middle of those beer cans and cigarette butts, rhodochrosite *heals abandonment. Heals emotional wounds.*

Once, I went to the rock store with my friend who knew exactly what she was looking for, and the necklace she bought had a huge round piece of the rock set in silver. It cost over a hundred dollars, and the chain was long enough to hang over her heart. I'd never seen money like that spent in that store before. I wanted it for her, the love she might get in exchange for all that cash. I wanted it for her like a prayer.

My only piece of rhodochrosite is the size of a button. It's set into silver, but tarnished and old. It was posted for sale on our neighbourhood message board for fifteen dollars, and I convinced my then-partner to buy it for me for Christmas. It means *love,* I told him, it represents *us.* He bought it, but left it shoved in some drawer on Christmas morning; forgot to give it to me until I asked, embarrassed. I could never bring myself to wear it after that. Our relationship ended, and the necklace became a relic, tied up in paper. It is still waiting for a new owner, for a birthday party, for someone to tell a better story about it.

My friend, on the other hand, did find love. A decade after we walked into that store, she conceived with a donor, and now that child has come into this world: pink and screaming, after a long, hard labour, like a prayer.

WHAT IS IT we are looking for in these crystals? Ourselves, I think. Earth as mirror, body as mimicry. Rhodochrosite looks like the idea of love, of recovery. Like a heart, or a womb, or a blood cell. When it's uncut, it's a pink glowing light emerging from black stone. Maybe we're saying: *I want that.* Maybe we're saying: *I want to be that.* It's a metaphor you can hold in your hand.

Is it more than a metaphor? Some people will tell you it stimulates circulation, helps reproductive organs. Who can say if they're wrong? Rhodochrosite has uses that are thousands of years old. Maybe hope quickens your pulse, or slows it. Maybe the stone is how you finally get out of bed. I believe faith has a deep role in healing. I believe there is power in prayer. And maybe this does it: your hope, your faith, your attention to the organs within you, flushes them with blood and oxygen, and they glow like rhodochrosite in the dark.

But the paradox is also there, glowing in the dark. We are told to be careful what we wish for, because we might receive it. What about what we pray *for*, and pray *with*? Maybe love formed these stones; the kind of love that is ore smashing ore into colour, over ten thousand years. Maybe rhodochrosite is the frequency of the earth touching itself into an act of creation: romance, pregnancy, blood, and circulation. Maybe we have read all the signs right. And still, the only way we can touch it is through violence.

I WANTED TO prove myself wrong. There are always shades to our choices, and I went looking for some. I found a $400 slice of rhodochrosite on Etsy, glowing pink, advertised as rare and ethical. It was sourced in Brazil. I didn't plan to buy it, but I hoped this one would be easier to trace; a rock that big, expensive, and apparently rare. "Could you tell me more about this?" I asked the seller.

She responded within five minutes: "It came from a very small deposit in Minas Gerais," she told me. "Likely found when something else was being mined…. These are purchased from small family-run mines or deposits. My suppliers only use mines they have visited or purchased the right to, so the workers are treated fairly."

For a few minutes after I read her answer, I felt relief. Maybe I'd gotten it wrong; maybe I could go back to the comfort I once felt, praying to those stones. But that feeling passed, the way an advertisement does, or a craving, because she had not told me the name of the company or the mine, or even what they were mining. She'd just said: *likely found when something else was being mined.* And too many possibilities remained in the space between my hope and her reassurance.

Rhodochrosite is not only found in Brazil; it is also found in Peru, South Africa, and Gabon, and each of these places have different mining histories and human rights records. Even if I take the vendor at her word, there is still a pressing social and environmental context that surrounds these mines. Minas Gerais is an inland state, filled with hundreds of high-risk tailing dams that rival the instability found in Cerro Rico. And like Potosí, these mines were established during the first waves of extractive colonialism—in this case, by the Portuguese colonial empire, circa 1500.

In the past decade, two large-scale disasters have taken place in Minas Gerais, resulting from dams breaking. Over fifty-five million cubic metres of tailing waste were spread in these floods; more than six hundred homes were destroyed, and close to three hundred people lost their lives.[4] To pray with rhodochrosite from these mines is to pray with the dams, as well; it's to seek love and compassion from the threshold of an imminent disaster.

Behind my DMs with the vendor: a world of wastewater, lying in wait.

BEYOND THE TAILING ponds in Minas Gerais: fresh water and estuaries, all worthy of prayer. At eighteen, I swam in a river in Chapada dos Guimãraes, in Mato Grosso, and that river ran all the way to Minas Gerais. The butterflies above me, my boyfriend talking loudly with his friends in Portuguese, all of us laughing and drunk. We found a waterfall and swam right behind it. There were crystals everywhere we walked. Back then, in 2003, President Luiz Inácio Lula had just been elected for his first term. "It's good," my boyfriend said. "Finally. We'll finally have democracy, you know?"

What did I know? Not very much. I was eighteen and in love for the first time, and I had never faced state violence. It was unlikely I ever would. There were wild horses at the farm where we stayed one weekend, and a scorpion in the shower. The power went out, and we smoked cigarettes around a single candle until dawn. That's what I picture when I think of Brazil: my boyfriend's long hair in the moonlight, the river we swam down, and all of the ways I learned the world is unfair.

Is that what I'll feel if I order the $400 stone? Beyond the tides in Minas Gerais, my own glowing place in the order of things,

which is a history of extraction. *Extraction.* That's what rhodochrosite looks like, when it's uncut: like you can still see the wall of
the cave, like you can see the moment they stole it. And this piece
on Etsy, it is the size of a heart. It looks like an organ stolen from
the wall of a mountain so we could find love, so we could heal
our harms.

It's been twenty years, and that boyfriend with long hair, Derich,
who killed the scorpion we found in our shower, still likes every
photo I post on Instagram. "YES," he says, "KEEP DOING YOU."
His hair isn't long anymore. Love changes, love carries on, and
some loves become a DJ. I am very happy for him. And DMs can
give us what rhodochrosite cannot: healing, memes, and unconditional love.

Diamond

From Greek adamas—*invincible, indestructible. A crystalline form
of pure carbon. The hardest known substance to naturally occur.
Known as a stone of strength and commitment.*

THERE IS A single diamond in my direct lineage. When I think
of Derich, and the way love gets tied to mining, I think of that
stone. My grandfather gave it to my grandmother when they
were married in the 1950s, and now that they have both passed,
my mother has the ring. The diamond is so small you can't
actually see it. Mostly you see where there is a setting for a tiny
gem, and I've been told it is a diamond. It's hard to imagine how
he afforded even that, given how poor they were. I imagine he
went hungry. I imagine he was saving for a long time. It's a work-
ing-class diamond, a poverty diamond, bought close to the time

De Beers transformed the world with their campaign: *a diamond is forever.*

This is the only diamond I have ever cared for. If my mother wanted to pass it down to me, I would cherish it, the way I cherish my nonna's scarves and my grandfather's dictionary. These are objects that hold both love and lineage. There are many stories of women immigrating from rural Calabria, like my nonna did in the 1940s, with rings and gems sewn into the hems of their dresses; heirlooms, dowries to pass on to generations to come. My grandmother's gold, my grandfather's invisible diamond: they act as dowry, inheritance, small marks of wealth within poverty. What they symbolize is not only love and lineage, but the complex work of survival.

What are a family's gems without their subtext? Not just context—but the stories buried within them. These rocks can carry a history of migration and loss; a secret language of maiden names and no-longer-spoken dialects. We touch the stone, and we touch what's left of a mother tongue, a mother country. But of course, we also touch the miner's hand, and the deep veins of silver and tin, diamond and amethyst, that run from Cerro Rico to Northern Ontario to Sierra Leone. We touch the fault line, the artery, where mines of the whole world meet.

A STONE IS easily disguised: by hand, by industry, by idea. Gemstones are too portable, too valuable, too difficult to extract and too costly to both human life and ecology to be marked *ethical* the same way as a textile. The earth has to be broken open. A person has to be placed inside a pit or a tunnel. And what is brought to the light can easily be moved to a new location before it is stamped with its place of origin. This versatility has always been the problem. It has been the solution, as well, for those seeking profit. When embargos, trade agreements, and public opinion have declared limits on where these resources can be sourced, industry has turned to literal sleights of hand. What cannot be placed in a pocket can be hidden in a policy, and what cannot be shrouded by policy can still be shaped by slogan—with crystals as with diamonds.

A diamond has only been *forever* since 1947, when De Beers told the world it was. When they launched their campaign, they held a monopoly on the world's diamond market and were seeking to widen demand and popularity. And it worked—it's said to have been one of the most successful campaigns in history. But their ads meant more than *your marriage will last*. De Beers' strategy—and continued monopoly—depended on maintaining and expanding their mining projects in places like Angola, South Africa, and Sierra Leone, at a time when African independence movements were mobilizing and fighting for liberation and sovereignty across the continent. Behind the slogan was a shadow line: *our diamond mines are forever. Our mining will go on.*

Their mining has gone on; a legacy of expansion, extraction, and branding. Love became closely associated with diamonds, even as De Beers—holding a monopoly so complete it was often called a cartel—spent decades funding, trading, and selling what became known as *blood diamonds*—a term reflecting the stone's role in outbreaks of acute violence, genocide, and civil war.[5] (For more on the complex history and ongoing legacy of De Beers— which reaches from Sierra Leone to Northern Ontario—see The Understory: "On Diamonds," page 223.)

A DIAMOND IS *forever. A crystal is for healing.* The mines of the Anthropocene, rich with symbols we call *love, power,* and *protection.* These are industries of symbol, with more than symbolism in common. The same machines dig the earth, and the same political machinery. Not all crystals come from diamond mines, but all diamond mines turn up crystals. All gold mines, all silver mines do, as well. Global Witness, the organization that first brought conflict diamonds to light, is actively conducting research into mining in Myanmar and Afghanistan, and they warn that as the market for healing crystals grows, so does its ability to fund—like diamonds did in Angola and Sierra Leona—insurgencies and civil war.[6]

This is the real cost; the real meaning of these stones. Not courage but corruption; not five dollars, but a life placed at risk. It's unlikely this will change. The reality is: for the crystal trade to become more transparent, the entire mining industry would have to become more transparent. And while crystals are a multi-billion-dollar industry, mining is a multi-*trillion*-dollar industry—it's the backbone, really, of all industry. It's how we make and remake the world.

Tourmaline

A complex boron silicate. Known as a stone for healing inner torment and dread. Used to aid in understanding oneself and others.

TOURMALINE IS ONE of the most colourful gemstones. It is a composite of silicate minerals that group together to form bright shades of blue, green, or purples. I own a single piece of tourmaline, and it is the only crystal I have ever received directly from a miner. I met him standing outside of Island Naturals, a health food store in Hilo, on the Big Island of Hawaii. He was around my age, sitting on the curb in cut-off jean shorts, holding an open jeweller's case filled with crystals. Small rough cuts in various colours, nestled there in blue velvet. It was 2012, and I was three months into living on the island, laughing with a few friends, drinking coconut water. I went right up to him. I talked to everyone back then, and I'd never seen crystals like that: all raw, uncut. Some of them looked like liquid that had suddenly frozen, others glittered like ice. I felt drawn to the stones the way I sometimes felt drawn to a stranger—like we could spend our lives together, or at least a few weeks.

"Tell me what these are," I said as I sat on the curb beside him, flirting with the stones. The crystals had come from a mine in Colorado, he told me, where he worked for a few months last summer. He'd gone there because he wanted to know where his crystals came from; he wanted to make sure they were ethical stones. The guy was almost handsome. His eyes were bright green, like the tourmaline in his case, and he held my gaze intensely. But he also looked rough: like he had been washing his clothes in the ocean; like the dirt from the mining camp was still on his jeans.

"I didn't last long," he told me. The conditions were bad in the camp and worse in the mine. His lungs hurt, his body hurt. He left after two months. I pictured him back there, in those red sand mountains, as he talked. He didn't want to take anyone's job— the other miners had families and people back home; many of them didn't have papers or residency either—so he didn't take a wage. He asked to be paid in crystals, instead; the rocks that sat between us in blue velvet, glittering in the hot sun.

"Are there any you feel drawn to?" he asked me, and I picked up the shard of green tourmaline. I felt like I could touch the mountain, like I could feel the cave wall. I asked him how much he wanted for it, but he shook his head. "I only do trades."

He looked like someone who could use the money, for food if nothing else. But I'd met people like him before: what money touched, they didn't want. He probably worked on one of the organic farms nearby, getting room and board for his labour, hitchhiking to town on occasion. I rummaged through my bag. The only thing I had was a small, handmade book of my poetry. It was printed and hand-sewn, the pages stitched together with thread. On the cover, I'd stamped a single bee. It didn't feel like enough, but I offered it. He looked at it for a while, then finally smiled. "Okay, then," he said, and gave me the crystal. "Take care of it."

"I will," I told him, and slipped the stone in my bra as I walked away. That's where I often kept them, close to my heart. But this one cut right into the skin. He wanted clean stones, cruelty-free stones—wanted them so badly, he'd gone down a shaft in the earth—and even that hadn't worked. There was still cruelty in it; dust he couldn't work from his jeans, from his lungs, from his life.

Lacuna

A small cavity, pit, or discontinuity; a blank space or missing part in a story. From Latin, lacuna: *hole, pit—figuratively: gap, void, want.*

THERE IS A lacuna, a cave, a hollow space that some of us feel in our lives. This space has to do with meaning, I think; it has to do with faith and the unsold world, the part of us that cannot be partitioned into currency, divided by hours. I feel it, at least: an absence that, like zero, cannot be held in your hands, divided, or ever fully explained, but that—paradoxically—wants to be known, tended, and seen. It is both exquisite and painful. It is what I was reckoning with in the rock store, I think. And maybe it's what drew that man I met down the mines.

Quartz and lapis, rhodochrosite and bloodstone: I bought them all in 2010, in the shadow of that lacuna. Making only three hundred dollars a week, racked by sadness, no clear way to explain my grief. Living off quinoa and lemon tap water, which I called a cleanse, instead of hunger. I hadn't met the miner yet. The tick had bit me that summer. I still thought the problem was a spider bite, *negative thinking*; I still hoped to pray away my nerve pain—the pain growing, rising through my cervical spine. I lay on the floor in my damp basement apartment, my personal cave, with citrine on my solar plexus to sooth my anger, and quartz on my forehead to stop my migraines. A large chunk of lapis lazuli— maybe traded by the Taliban, though I didn't know it—on my swollen thyroid.

There is a lacuna, a *gap*, *void*, *want*—that is ineffable, that has to do with meaning. And there is also a lacuna that has to do with literal gaps, discontinuities between what we need, and what we have. It is a benefit to many systems when we pray to small, cheap chips of the earth for our fundamental needs. I needed medicine, I wanted connection, and I was told crystals might heal the chasm I felt. In the absence of health care and a living wage, in the absence of government support, I relied on a handful of stones.

Faith is not a placebo; we can survive on it, when we have little else. Lying on the basement floor, hope carried me through winter, once my credit card was maxed. So it doesn't surprise me: crystal sales rising in the wake of the pandemic. Diamonds might be a luxury, but crystals are branded for *healing*, and even economists understood that as they watched the crystal market rise. Alone in our homes, isolated and still at risk: we couldn't touch one another, but we could touch the same stones for courage, at least. Rose quartz, amethyst: stones of power, recovery. More than that, most of all: we had entered a sudden nightmare of health together. And, like most nightmares, there were no rules for what would happen next. No saying who would appear, suddenly transformed. Around every corner: *another fucking disaster.* And here it is: medical resources become scarcer and scarcer. Your country tells you to do whatever you can to avoid the hospital, do whatever you can to stay home. We cannot help you unless you are *critical*, they say, and if you are *critical*, it may be too late. And maybe, your country is also the United States, so illness and bankruptcy go nicely together, and in your dreams and also in waking life, no one wears masks.

It's not shameful to be desperate. It's not shameful to want to be safe. The work of survival is never simple, we do the best we can with our grief. And still, the paradox: we may need to do better. If our prayer is to remake this world, to build between us something that can sustain life —and even hold justice—we may need to turn elsewhere. I'm not here to shame how anyone else prays; I only know my own way to God, and what I call God is something ineffable, something that does not really fit that word. We are deep, and varied, and essentially good, I believe, like all beings. But working with crystals, with the industry as it is, may always be shrouded; you may never be able to see all the turns. Which is fitting, I guess, because that's what they are: parts of the world that did not grow to be witnessed. The deep veins, the rare rocks of the underground: they are the earth speaking to itself in the dark. So maybe it's best to pray to our own clean breath in the air. To sit on some patch of city dirt and remember that there are always crystals beneath us. Under the sewers, below the clay and unbroken earth, there is a world of quartz ever growing, ever glowing, in the dark.

Black Kyanite

An aluminum-rich silicate stone. Forms under extremely high pressure. Used as a stone of protection.

RIGHT AND WRONG, true and false—binaries make a story easier to manage, easier to explain. I want it to be like that with gem-stones, but it isn't. Crystals are a nexus where money meets spirit, where the ineffable calls to us and violence responds: we want God and we find a tailing pond; we seek medicine and the rock we get is the rock of a graveyard. The complete devastation of it. I thought it was spirit responding. For years, I talked to a god I did not know was covered in dynamite, that could have cost a man his life.

These stones are different from other ore; different from the lithium in our phones—we might base our lives around both—but prayer here is not an analogy. They told us *heal thyself* at this alter, *commit* a vow to this stone. These are the bricks of the church. Rose quartz for love. Jasper for wealth. Kyanite for *please God, protect me.* We placed the stones in our pillowcases, in our bras, on our bodies, left them in our water to mineralize what we drank. We drank the water, we healed, and what it cost was five dollars, and what it cost was the earth.

Betrayal. Over and over again. From *betray* (verb): to lead astray, to fail or desert especially in a time of need. Synonym: bad faith. As in: another tailing pond in Minas Gerais breaks through its dam, as the rhodochrosite is risen to light. *Give me compassion,* we will say to that stone, and we will mean it. We will be good and loving, and holding a broken piece of the earth that cannot be returned or repaired. We do the best we can with our grief. We do the best we can when we are lied to. What do we do with the truth?

THE TRUTH IS, I broke a vow to myself. I bought another stone this winter: a jagged piece of black kyanite. I bought it knowing some of what I know now—not everything, but enough to understand the stone's label of *ethically sourced* didn't mean much. It was January, ice-cold, and most stores were closed because of the pandemic. So I stood in a mask on the sidewalk in front of the enormous new rock store, with its big windows and two stories, and the store clerk handed me a wrapped paper parcel through a small open window. I didn't touch the rock until I got home, when I could unravel the tissue paper in private. Then I ran it under cold water, and placed it into a bowl of salt. The ritual felt good, like rolling a cigarette back when I smoked. It felt familiar and safe, and that's what I needed—safety—that's why I made the choice. Not casual safety. I was trying to find an alternative to calling the police.

Black kyanite is said to be a grounding stone, a stone of protection. Did I believe the stone would protect me? I wasn't sure—but I did not believe the police would. The work of survival is never simple, and I wanted everyone involved to survive. So, I hedged my morals; I went back to the crystal store. I prayed to that rock that night. I prayed to it for hours. Woke with salt in my hair and marks on my skin where the stone had left an impression; I'd slept with it pressed to my heart. *I am protected*, I told the kyanite. *You are protected*, the kyanite told me.

How badly I needed that; how few objects could have given that to me. I understand why I broke my ethics against my fear. The problem is not simply that we are turning to small shards of the earth to fulfil our basic human needs; it's that we might have to. When we face imminent threats, we take imminent measures. But I would rather pray to an unbroken mountain. I know that with certainty now. I would rather touch the bare skin above my heart, and lay myself down in the sun to catch heat. When spring came, I buried that kyanite in the back yard. It did not belong there, but there was symmetry in what I did.

UNDERTOW
(water)

Between the idea
And the reality
Between the motion
And the act
Falls the Shadow

—T.S. Eliot, "The Hollow Men"

HURRICANE'S EYE

I.

THREE STARFISH LAY in Jay's hands like bright flowers: red, orange, purple. I could see them pulsing, moving slightly, trying to breathe air. "Thank you," I said, since I'd asked him to get them, since I stupidly wanted to see them up close. I didn't know it could hurt them to touch them. I didn't know a lot of things. Just how to stand there in the sunlight, a quarter-in-love, with the hostel to my left, the ocean to my right, and the laughter between us. Jay waded back into the ocean to set them free and I put my feet in the bright water. We ate the barracuda he'd caught that night, and stared at each other a bit, while the people around us dealt cards and some British guy tried to play Oasis on an out-of-tune guitar. There was no internet, no computer in the hostel. Just a few old couches, some bunk beds, and a radio that someone remembered to check for the weather. There was a storm coming. A day, maybe two days away. Most of us didn't care, but one girl packed up her things and got on the first boat in the morning. "It's a storm," she said, "a tropical storm." It wasn't even an island we were on, just a caye, a few miles of rock. We laughed when she left. We laughed at any dumb tourist who packed up and left, just because a hurricane might hit.

II.

WHAT USE IS a story that ignores its fault lines? Very little is reliable in this, except for the starfish. They were taken from the ocean and returned. The bakery had hardly any bread, once the storm was truly there, and I bought what they had left for the hostel. As for the rest? The plates of my memory shift, like a rift under that island. I stopped writing this story, over and over. Hit by vertigo, like the storm was back at my window. A halo of guilt, a migraine of shame—something here doesn't want to be remembered. A fault line, maybe? Or an undertow. There is a perfect sunset in this story, spent sitting on a rooftop with Jay. I don't want to analyze us kissing, I mean really, *maybe we just liked each other*. The way you like someone beautiful and kind. Fault line, current: I know it's never that simple. There was an estuary, not far from that hostel, where the fresh water mixed with the sea. And a split, called *the split*, where a hurricane once broke the caye in two pieces. A picnic table was perched in it. You could sit there and drink beer, between the island and the island, and the sea.

III.

WE WANTED TO go out, whether or not a storm was coming. There was a good bar, Emma said, and people would still be there; only the idiots had left. And if they hadn't left yet, they couldn't leave now, because the boats weren't running anymore. So whoever was on the island would be at the bar, and the bar played good music until late. Emma knew things. She had grey-white hair and a sacred left hand, activated back home in Scotland. It could move heat, it could heal, it could make things happen, including free drinks. We loved each other from the first moment we met, like we'd been friends across many lifetimes, and here was a life where we could sit on the beach, together again. We spent our days in the split, talking about the visions that often hit us in the face, both of us on a cliff of manic, but is manic even manic when you're this in love, this in tune with the water moving around you? She'd been there two months already, living on fruit and reading the irises of tourists. Not for money, just to see the pattern, the path, how life was moving for them. When she looked in my eyes, she saw her own, and I saw mine in hers, which was just like a mirror facing a mirror: it goes on forever, it never ends. She watched Jay bring me those starfish. "He loves you," she told me. "You know that, right?" That morning, her and I had been standing in the shallows, eating our breakfast which was a bottle of beer, and someone had come up to us with a five-gallon jar filled with water. In that jar were seahorses. I'd never seen seahorses before. Over and over, we told each other and anyone who would listen, *the male seahorse is the mother, you know. The male seahorse will carry the baby. The male seahorse gives birth.* We got to the bar by eleven. We couldn't leave earlier because there was so much singing and laughing to do, to make the orbit around us spin like the orbit within us. "You're so beautiful," she kept telling me, "like Sophia Loren." Not with desire; she said it like a mirror facing a mirror, and pointed to the well-built man sitting by the bar, and then she went off dancing, barefoot, the floor of that bar just sand and cigarette butts. You could see the glitter around her, not an aura but a sparkler that would not burn out, and I promised myself I'd be just like that at forty, as I went and sat by that well-built blond.

IV.

IS IT COMMON to black out when you write about a blackout? Something here doesn't want to be remembered; something persists. I planned to write about the hurricane that nearly hit us, I didn't want to write the rest. There are complex implications of power on the rooftops in this story, and two rooftops, at least. I spent weeks on that caye, high sun burning whatever childhood names I had left. Sitting on the dock, I saw a stingray jump from the ocean, fly across the surface for a nautical mile. It doesn't seem right, that they can fly like that. So maybe I have the memory wrong, like how many others? The starfish went back to the sea—I know that. All I could get was a candle and two loaves of bread to get us through the storm, and we pooled what we had together, including our pity for ourselves, which we called adventure. When I say *complex implications of power*, I mean I would never pretend sex is neutral, I know that it's not. When tourists say *leave no trace*, what do they think neocolonialism is? I mean, really: we leave a mark. And I am the same as any, maybe with more visions, more self-contempt that goes away when I'm drunk. Speaking of complex, that well-built blond was a British Royal Marine, and my blackout was a blackout on the roof of his hotel—or was it in his bed?

V.

"HE WENT DOWN on me underwater," I told Emma. It was the last thing I could remember. His hotel had a Jacuzzi on the roof, and you could see the entire island, rising from the sea. Just lights at night, really. He was there on the island with his buddies. They were stationed on a ship nearby, all marines who knew how to dive for a living, and they had come here to dive the famous Blue Hole. They weren't leaving for a storm. They weren't leaving until they conquered that dive. There's not much else I remember— not his voice, or his laughter—just that one flashing moment, realizing how well he could hold his breath underwater, my utter surprise, and then nothing. It was an expensive hotel, where I woke up in the morning. I was in a white robe. Emma laughed when I told her, and I laughed, and we went looking for bread and bottled water because the storm was truly coming by then. We saw him eating fruit with his shirtless friends at the café on the beach, but I couldn't look at him, a knot in my stomach, my vertigo rising, I just kept walking. "He loves you," Emma said. "You should have seen how he looked at you, Sophia Loren, just wow."

VI.

WE BATTENED DOWN the hatches. I learned what that meant: every piece of wood was nailed down to other pieces of wood to keep the windows shut, so the building and us might survive. We stayed together in one room, the seven of us still at the hostel, the four kids living on the property, and Jay who was their uncle. Emma braided everyone's hair. She lit candles like it was a ceremony, and the wind blew so hard it was clear the house would fall down with all of us laughing inside, still laughing at the tourists who left: *wimps, do they even know what it's like to really travel?* And no, it turned out, the house was not going to fall, though for an hour I thought of my family back home like a prayer. We shared the bread and the water and the rum and began to look beautiful as we got drunk, and the wind died to silence, and Emma said, "The eye. It's the eye." I'd never heard silence like that. We went out in our dresses, down to the beach. Checked out the bar where my drink might've been spiked the night before, but no one was dancing, just a red plastic bag was moving over rocks, and we shrugged. *Worth a try.* No one slept. We drew our mattresses into a circle and waited until a god-hand of thunder returned and hit the roof of the house like a sermon. Until dawn, it went on, until morning and beyond. That rattle on the roof the rattle of a world falling down, and I thought, *will we make it?* and I thought, *what a story this story will be.*

THE ROMANCE
OF FLOODS

CUIABÁ IS HOT and humid. The kind of hot that can make you dizzy, a humid that sticks to your clothes. Some days we went to the mall to escape the heat, and smoked Marlboros in the air-conditioned corridors. Mostly, my friends and I waited for night, or the rare fall of rain. On days when the sky broke, it broke hard enough to tear through your clothing. There would be some warning before it happened: a stillness beneath the stillness. A complete absence of wind that could last for an hour or a day. But I knew it was time when the thunder started. If I was in the market, I would have to wade home against a current, the streets filled so quickly. On those days, we didn't wait for night. We sat on the porch with our feet sticking out in the water and ate rice, played cards, felt ourselves able to move faster without the weight of the heat.

Derich told me that the city drowned once. He said caimans from the wetlands swam downstream and ate the wreckage. I pictured the scene without anyone in it, without the walls of people's homes folding like wet paper. In the vision, the slick backs of the caimans slid through the new rivers and the city was silent, windless. Everyone had left. How did they leave? I didn't ask. I wanted to believe there was romance in the flood.

But there was nothing romantic about it. The flood had taken place only two years before. In six hours, the city received months' worth of rain, and water rose ten feet high in the streets. Some were evacuated to safety in helicopters, while others were forced to remain.[1] It was less poetic than this, too. A writer facing words is not a person facing nature. Water climbed up my ankles, not my thighs, when it rained in Cuiabá. And if a flood had begun during my visit, rushing through the streets, I would have found a way to leave.

I MET DERICH a few days after I arrived in Brazil. He was standing by a tree in the courtyard of a bar, and I was halfway through a bottle of sugarcane rum. I had just been grabbed and kissed by a guy with a large tattoo of Jesus on his shoulder. It was an unexpected, unwelcome kiss. So I was avoiding the group I'd come with, drinking cachaça in a dark corner alone. Derich was an English teacher and had hair down to his shoulders. He played electric guitar, he told me. And when I started swaying, he took away my bottle and returned me to my friends.

When I woke up the next day, he was there. We were both fully dressed, sharing my twin bed. The sun was blinding and my head pounded. I wasn't sure how I'd gotten home, and even under a cold shower, I could not remember his name. I didn't ask. It seemed unforgivable to ask. We were inseparable from then on, though. He spent every night at the volunteer house where I lived, and brought me to his grandmother's place for dinner. We went to the pool hall with his friends, and he said my name proudly, stretching out the centre: Alessssandra.

This is what it's like to fall in love, I thought. I had never been in love before. I was eighteen years old and had just finished high school. I'd known him less than a week and I still wasn't sure of his name. *Love,* I called him. *Babe,* I called him. Then, sitting on the porch some nights later, I called him *a local.* I don't remember what came before that. I remember the heat, the brightness around us—so much sun—and the way he cringed. "*Gringa,*" he replied, and took his hand off my knee.

We stared at the skyline for a long time, saying nothing. Then we went to the market to drink *licuados,* passing through an alley where twelve kids were once found murdered, Derich told me. "It was probably the police," he said.

That night he carved our names into a city bench. *Derich Da Costa. Alessandra Naccarato.* But I called him *De-rich* for a week before he corrected me. "Der-ick," he said gently. "It's Derich."

I LIVED IN the volunteer house with three other people, each from a different country: Wales, Germany, England. Together, we were a map of *gap years,* shoddy development aid. We were supposed to be teaching English and helping with a vague clean water mission, but the projects were all on pause. The ex-pat director of the program was in a divorce battle with his Brazilian wife. He didn't want to leave her anything, apparently; he'd already gotten another woman pregnant, apparently. I learned all of this after I arrived. One of the other volunteers, Mary, picked me up from the airport, stinking of rum. "The project is basically a scam," she said once we got home, then handed me a bottle of beer. "Cheers."

There wasn't much we had to do, so we went to concerts and the mall. We drank and hung out on the porch with our friends from the neighbourhood who had a rock band. Derich played lead guitar. We drove out of town to someone's aunt's house, in a borrowed car, and at dawn I realized there were wild horses around us. The guys set up a drum kit and amps on the porch. There was rainforest all around us, it didn't matter how loud they played, only the jungle heard us. And it went on like that for months. I adopted a stray kitten that Derich planned to keep. Mary paid for everyone's drinks: *the British pound being what it is.* But then Mary started dating Derich's best friend, who was eighteen like me. She was thirty. "He's fine with it," she told me.

And then a month later, lying in the hammock, half cut, she told me she'd decided to get pregnant. "He's fine with it," she said again.

STRUCTURAL VIOLENCE. That's what I think of when I remember our volunteer house: Mary in the hammock, myself trying to remember Derich's name. Mary was pregnant when she left Cuiabá. Her daughter would be eighteen now. And from what I've heard, they never returned.

WHEN I LEFT Cuiabá I pretended, just for a moment, that none of it had happened. What proof did I have? Legs ballooned with insect bites and a single earring made of chicken feathers. I sat on the plane before takeoff and flipped the thought like a coin: *I did.*

I didn't. It was. It wasn't. We had parked on the side of the highway to watch the underbellies of planes. I could still smell Derich on me. But if I wanted, I could pretend it was the sweat of sleep, that I had woken where I fell asleep three months before.

A few weeks later, I called Derich from Rio and his grandmother answered. In badly worded Portuguese, I told her I would call again soon. But then I drank coconut water and walked barefoot through Ipanema, staring off at the ocean. When I finally phoned, Derich was returning from the airport. "My grandmother said you were coming," he told me. He'd driven out there, spent six hours at the arrival gate, waiting. "When are you coming back?" he asked me. I didn't have an answer. "I love you," I said instead.

I left for Canada the next day. There was sand and salt in my hair from the ocean, but I didn't rinse it out, I wanted to bring what I could with me. At the airport, security guards were everywhere, and crowds hurried through the gates. *I've forgotten something,* I thought, as I checked my suitcase. When I boarded the plane, I remembered. We rose into the sky, and I tried not to think about it. Below me, the continent stretched out. I studied the land underneath me, ridged and unbroken. I wanted to see the Pantanal from above; the wetland where the caimans lived. Maybe I would return soon, after all. Maybe my life was veering, just being written. My period was at least a week late. What would my life look like at nineteen? I flipped the thought like a coin: terrifying, beautiful. Devastating. I thought of Mary, and the screaming match we had when she finally told me she was pregnant.

"How could you do this to him?" I'd shouted.

"I love him," she'd yelled back.

I let the world narrow to the green beneath me—that, only

that—as the plane flew on. And then, I saw it beneath me: the wetland that could flood Cuiabá, like Derich said. Green and marked with pools of water. It kept going, and going. The largest wetland in the world, reaching all the way to Santa Cruz in Bolivia, the size of half of Europe. It went on like freedom, like choice, like the possibilities of my future. It was beautiful. It didn't look like it could do any harm.

A BRIEF HISTORY
OF MERMAIDS

AT MERMAID PONDS, we climb a seacliff of obsidian. Andrew leads the way, crossing a gap to the rockface when the tide pulls out. He doesn't offer me his hand, and I don't ask for it. I follow him barefoot, feeling the sharp edges of the hardened lava cut into my feet. The ledge we finally reach is jagged, wet, and covered in barnacles—it's barely a ledge at all. And looking down, I realize we're surrounded by water now. The tide has grown stronger, filled the shallow ponds beneath us, the lacuna we crossed. We're twelve feet up, and the ocean looks like it could surge up and greet us. The ocean looks like the only thing there is. Blue meets blue in the distance, there is no horizon line. *We're on the edge of the world,* I think, *and it does have a cliff after all.*

Less than a mile out, I notice a difference in the waves. I've learned to read the pattern, I know what will happen, but there is still no way to prepare: a whale is a miracle every time. The tail grazes the surface. "Look," I point, as it sinks beneath, gathering momentum. And then the humpback rises, breaching the surface, heaving most of its body into the air.

Andrew has never seen this before: a whale rising and crashing, and rising again, the ocean declaring its secret to the sky. And there's more than one, the ocean is alive with them: a whole pod, playing and breeching. Andrew is laughing and whooping beside me, and I keep hearing myself say *yes*. A single, unequivocal word: *yes*.

I've been afraid of the ocean for most of my life. Terrified, even. You become part of the water when you enter it, and no one can say for how long. But something has been changing in me. The ocean is wild. The whales are of that same wild, the kind that clashes against itself just to remember delight. I want the same thing to wake in me. That's what I'm doing with Andrew on this cliff. That's why I've been throwing myself into the waves down the road, at a beach called *Kehena*—a Hawaiian word for hell—where people often drown. I used to stay on the beach, never let my feet lift in the water. But these days I dive forward, I plunge under, I open my eyes. You have to want something more than you are afraid of it. It just took me a long time to want it this bad.

I am standing on the narrow ledge now. Twelve feet down, the waves hit the rock with enough strength to break bone. I know I should sit back down, but I can see something else moving in the water below us. Andrew laughed when I told him why I wanted to come to this place. "It's just a name," he said. Another person would call the figure seaweed, barracuda, maybe a shark. They would be content to watch the whales and lean back into Andrew's arms. But I am not another person.

•

IF YOU GO looking for the origins of mermaids, you'll often hear the same thing: sailors mistook the shape of manatees for women. But that story ignores millennia of faith. The world over, we've believed in a woman beneath the sea. And throughout history, we've brought her offerings: sacrifices, stories, even our dead. Children still sing to her, laughing, dressed in her image. Ariel, Atargatis, the nereids in Greece, the selkies in Scotland, the lonely bronze statue of the Little Mermaid off the shore in Copenhagen: mermaids are alive between us, if not beneath us. And our faith in them has a fossil record: fish bones scattered, forgeries buried in the ground, plastic toys piled in landfills, washing back out to sea. There is so much we will never know about the ocean, so little we control. And the mermaid loves us, tricks us, drowns us, saves us—the mermaid guides us through that unknown.

•

THE FIRST MERMAID I fell in love with was Daryl Hannah. We couldn't afford to go to the video store often, so my father laboured to copy *Splash* off TV, pausing the recording at every commercial break. I watched the movie over and over, holding my breath as it started, waiting for Daryl Hannah's crimped hair, her naked arrival on land, surrounded by gawking humans. Cut screen to Tom Hanks, young and sad in the city, unaware he's about to fall in love with a creature of the sea.

Young as I was, with my home-cut bangs and inexhaustible

imagination, *Splash* was the first love story I believed in. But it wasn't the love between them I cared about, it was whatever that woman had with the ocean. I watched her hide herself in human legs and department store clothing, afraid of being found out. Confused and astonished by the world, breaking TV screens with the pitch of her voice. I waited for the moment she would lock the door to the bathroom and sink into the tub, her orange tail unfurling, the look on her face perfectly content. I had never seen the ocean, except on a screen. I imagined it would be both beautiful and terrifying to encounter, to touch in real life—something like visiting the moon. I was relieved when she finally returned there, to the place where she belonged. But it never seemed quite right that Tom Hanks went with her. He was conflicted, still wearing a suit jacket, forced to jump in after her. I wanted to follow instead. To be there with her, daughterlike, in the glowing ocean. Would I be terrified? *Yes.* But I also might discover I belonged.

Back in those days, we often took the streetcar down to Harbourfront, and stood by the lake. In good weather, we'd take the ferry across to the Toronto Islands. At the far side of Ward's Island, facing away from the city, Lake Ontario stretches as far as you can see. Blue meets blue in the distance; the horizon line sometimes disappears. They would fly a green flag on the beach when the water tested clean enough, and my mother would let us swim. I would think of Daryl Hannah as I waded in, and a trill would run through me.

"Open your eyes," my sister would tell me, collecting smooth rocks from the bottom. "You have to open your eyes if you want to find them." She was fearless, and strong, and would do handstands in the water—her top half submerged in the lake, her legs sticking straight out, like some kind of reverse mermaid. But I never opened my eyes. Part of me feared I would find something twisted and magical down there; part of me feared that I wouldn't. Maybe this is where forgeries and mermaid hoaxes come from: our desire for evidence, and our fear of it.

•

BEFORE I WENT to the Mermaid Ponds with Andrew, when I was still in Canada and getting ready for my trip, I saw a clickbait article: "Mind-Blowing Mermaid Found at the Beach of Hawaii." How could I not click? The images weren't like any I'd seen before. In these, she was pale and swollen, dead on the shore. Her figure was enormous and gruesome, and her tail had thick arterial veins across it. I couldn't look away from what I'd seen. I pictured her over and over: lying on the black sand beach, not far from where I'd once watched lava pour into the sea. If a mermaid was going to beach herself, that seemed like a likely place. Between the depth in the picture, her ugliness, my own willingness to believe: she was real, I thought, or a stunning forgery. Not some Photoshop mock-up—this was a forgery done by hand—and I couldn't stop picturing the artist. Can you see him?

Light filters in, through the rag he's tacked over the window. He's been in the shed since six a.m., trying to avoid the heat. But the sun is high now, filling the room with warmth and light. He'll lock up soon, leave it for evening. It's hard to pull himself away, though, when the figure is so close to perfect. He's down to the intricate details: smoothing, perfecting the wax ridges, the scales. And now the light is landing on her face. The way the shadow falls, it looks like she's sleeping, like she just might open her eyes.

•

IN FIFTH GRADE, I finally saw the ocean. Our relatives flew us to the coast to visit, something our parents never could afford. And one morning, we headed to an inlet at dawn. My aunt carried a canoe with the help of my mother, as we climbed down the slick rocks to the shore. The mist was so thick you could barely see the water. My sister and I clipped on orange life jackets and sat in the gently rocking boat as the women launched it forward.

We glid through the water and I thought of my favourite book, an old worn copy of *The Seal Mother* by Mordicai Gerstein. In the story, there is a seal who sheds her skin and comes to land as a beautiful woman, to dance and sing on the summer solstice. But a fisherman steals her pelt and hides it, forcing her to stay on land. The bargain he strikes is for marriage: she will become his wife for seven years, and then he will let her return to the sea. But when the time comes, he refuses. It's her son who has to find the hidden pelt and finally set her free.

Selkie stories come from Scotland and Ireland, and our mother comes from a line of Irish women. And sometimes she told us different selkie stories as we fell asleep, ones she seemed to pull from memory. So there was no saying, really, what would happen once we entered the bay; if our mother might finally go free.

Dawn was breaking around us, I remember, pink and red in the sky. It was deeply quiet. And then with a splash, the first seal surfaced, so close to the boat I could reach out and touch it. Then another, and another. The ocean was full of them.

"Look," my mother said, and as the fog parted, I saw a small island ahead. A dozen seals were resting there in the cool morning air, waiting for the July sun to rise. My mother smiled, tracing one hand in the cold water. We had come to the seal's place, their water-land, and it was part of our world after all.

IS IT SURPRISING that I moved there, decades later? When I thought I was ready to settle down, I moved across the country, to an island not far from that inlet. And I would wake before sunrise to go to the shore and see what was hidden in the mist. So I get it, Tom Hanks, why you followed Daryl Hannah in the end; I get why you loved her from the moment you met—I did, too.

•

LOVE AFFAIRS WITH sea creatures rarely go well; there is always a sacrifice required. In many stories of Atargatis, who is often called the oldest-known mermaid, she is a goddess who falls in love with a shepherd, and accidently causes his death. In her grief, she drowns herself in a lake. But instead of dying, she transforms into a fish. And her beauty is such that it cannot be hidden, so she maintains part of the body of a woman.

Atargatis was stamped on coins, carried to Greece, and Rome, and further—her stories shifting like her body to become a tangle of myth. It is difficult to trace her, but most agree she became Derketo in Greece, and some say Aphrodite and Venus as well. There is a part of her, maybe, in every mermaid story we now tell. An echo of her in selkies, nereids—even Mélusine, who is now stamped on Starbucks cups.[1]

Atargatis, transfigured by water; Atargatis, transfigured by grief. If this is where the story of the mermaid begins, then it begins with heartbreak and sacrifice, with beauty and a cost to pay. That part of the story never ends. But why would it? If you've lived near the ocean or a lake, you know how it is: you become part of the water when you enter it, and no one can say for how long.

•

WHEN I WAS thirteen, I saw the ocean again. I travelled with two friends to Sweden and Denmark. The trip was a kind of luxury I hadn't experienced before, growing up with powdered milk and parents who made art for a living. But we went to visit a friend—a former exchange student—whose family was wealthy enough to cover most of the costs. On a bright day in Copenhagen, we all went down to the water. A crowd was gathered there, looking at a bronze statue offshore. It was a life-size girl sitting on a rock, looking infinitely sad. "It's the Little Mermaid," our friend's father told us. "This is the city where the story was written."

Then he recalled what he knew of Hans Christian Andersen's story: the mermaid gave up her tongue for a set of legs. She danced, even though it was like dancing on knives. For all she sacrificed, she still wasn't loved. And in the end, she threw herself into the sea.

I looked over the water. I studied the look on the statue's face, so much like mine. Young as I was, depressed as I was, in a way that went beyond so-called teenage angst. Burgeoning into existential, into the kind of heartbreak you never recover from. I was trying to make sense of the world I lived in, but how could I? I felt like I was dancing on knives. The world doesn't have room for all of you when you're a teenage girl. That's how I felt. It asks you to show up with part of your body, part of your personality, your desire. To compartmentalize as your body thrums with hormones, fashions itself into something alien and strange. Back then, I wanted to unmake myself completely, to become as insignificant as seafoam. It had nothing to do with romance. It had to do with unbelonging, with a sense I didn't fit in the world I was in. Like I'd grown up with two legs, when what I needed was a fin. If there'd been a sea witch to ask, I would have made the trade.

WHEN I CAME home, I read the full story. I was starting grade nine at a new school, trying to fit my body into small clothing, dieting and taking drugs that made me feel underwater.

"I know well enough what you want," the sea witch says, when the mermaid comes to her. "It'll hurt, it'll be like a sharp sword going through you."

I put a picture of the statue on my wall, in a cheap wood frame. I dyed my hair dark red. "So be it," the mermaid responds to the witch. "So be it." And then she gives up her tongue.

The moral of the story, I thought to myself, *is that the world is fucking unfair.* But I was glad someone had finally said it. Life isn't fair when you're a teenage girl. Life isn't fair when you're Hans Christian Andersen either, apparently: it's said he wrote the story for a man he loved, when that man was married to a woman.[2] He's the mermaid in the story, many say, ready to surrender his voice. No wonder I found it so relatable.

It was good to have a place to put my grief; it was good to have some company. I wasn't so alone in my loneliness, the story told me, I wasn't so alone in my heartbreak at this world—the world was heartbroken, too. There was a hidden story in the fable as well, an undercurrent, and some part of me could see that, no matter how depressed I was: A world gets heartbroken because it knows how to love.

There's no apathy in the ocean, in *The Seal Mother*, in *The Little Mermaid*. Atargatis, it turns out, is a goddess of protection.

Andersen was eventually buried beside the man that he loved. And the Little Mermaid did not cast herself to the sea. In Andersen's original story, she was given a silver blade and a choice: "Make haste! He or you must die before the sun rises." And even facing her death, she does not choose violence. She casts the dagger away. And though she expects to become seafoam—though that was her bargain—because she's been selfless, she's remade instead: transformed, transfigured, and claimed by the Daughters of the Air. So she wasn't on that shore in Copenhagen, after all; she was everywhere.

·

WHAT DO WE make of a power that is beyond us? One that can easily decide if we live or die; one that is indivisible, unmappable, never fully seen by the naked eye? You could call that force God, or you could call it the ocean. Some of us want to honour it, some of us want to conquer it, some of us want to use it as a mirror. Maybe all three, maybe more; maybe we want to feel our own surrender. There is grace in how small we are, how vulnerable, to the immensity of water. Can you know yourself without relationship? Without aspect ratio? What is true in my life becomes much clearer at the shore, including the truth of how little I know. Faith gets me through, when all else fails, when the boat of my life is down to its last fresh water. The unknown will always be unknown, that is its very essence. The known expands, the truth remains: we are *vincible*, a single exhale, and water is stronger than iron.

From those unspeakable depths, from that wild unknown, from the god-mouth of the ocean: a tangled body, a hybrid body emerges. We are mostly water, and they are mostly *mer*. We might drown at any moment: at sea, or in the pneumonia of our own lungs, or in the kiddie pool at Disneyland, so it makes sense to pray: *O' God, O' Atargatis, O' nereid, O' figure on the mast, O' mermaid, O' selkie, O' Hans Christian Andersen*: protect us from ourselves. Give us safe passage through the unknown. We've built a continent of garbage in the South Pacific. It has gathered by current into a single floating land, and the whales can't hear themselves think, let alone find their way out of the mall of tankers. *What will come?* It would be a comfort, if you could tell us, mermaid. It would be a comfort if you could speak. If you were willing to consider, say, a trade.

IT MAKES SENSE to me: wanting a guide, a presence, something to bargain with in the sea. Living on islands for years, I often heard about drownings. You'd be at the shore in the morning, or you'd swim out to a dock in the lake. And then by nightfall, someone would have lost their life there. In small communities, loss like that is intimate. You often know the person's name, or their cousin, or their wife, and the story is repeated—as a warning, as an honouring. Once, at a lake just down the hill from my house, two tourists drowned in the lily pads. They were only ten feet from shore. No one was there, no one could say exactly what happened. How do you reckon with a loss like that? I pictured something that lived in those weeds, and I couldn't say if it would have helped them or harmed them. I couldn't say, thinking of those tourists, that I understood the powers of this world.

Love, and loss, and love again. It took me some time, but I swam in the lake again, where the tourists drowned. Don't we always? Past the lily pads, out into the cold open centre, where an old dock floated in the sun.

•

WHEN I ARRIVED on the Big Island, my luggage full of dresses and camping gear, all I could think of was the mermaid corpse. I'd only been gone from the island for two months. "Something called me back," I told my friends, and they nodded. What called me back was depression. So deep and heavy, I was in bed for months, beached, unable to slide back into the water, even though it was an arm's reach away. In those dry months, I relied on other people's imagination, bad TV, long fantasy novels. I was looking for a way back to faith.

When faith happens, it is difficult to explain why or how. The mermaid looked like something I could believe in. The world had made her, or someone who believed fiercely in the magic of the world, and this knowledge helped me get out of bed. The world is not so simple, she told me. It cannot be categorized into sadness and joy. It is massive, inexplicable, and grows exponentially when we admit how little we know.

Maybe this is the work of the forger: to create space for faith. And it's not a hoax, then, it's not a forgery at all. It's art, it's an offering, an act of worship. Can you see him?

It's the middle of the night. The bare lightbulb is flickering above him, and he stands over the mermaid, studying it. It's done. Any more work might ruin it, and he's ruined enough of his paintings to know. The sculpture took longer than any canvas; he's been working on her for years. Collecting animal bones and stripping fish, experimenting with wax and polymers. Going hungry, even, to afford the supplies. All to recreate what he'd seen that day at Kehena: swimming near Tahiti Rock, without fins or a mask—a stupid thing to do on any day, especially with the tiger shark hanging around—and then the surf woke up, waves cresting ten feet high before they crashed down. He tried to get in, swam right into an undertow, then a riptide, and he knew it was over. Pulled under, he saw the shark, he saw the ten-foot barracuda everyone was talking about, then he saw a glimmer. And it wasn't, it turned out, the glimmer of his death. He heard the word swim, *and he knew which direction to turn. A few minutes later, he was safely on shore.*

The next day, he started sketching. And now she was done. The last step was to let her go. He would go tonight, down to the Mermaid Ponds. Drive down through the grove, and carry her through the woods, down the volcanic steps. The moon was high enough, there'd be light. He already knew which pond he'd choose, where he'd leave the offering, glistening in the moonlight. The tide crashing over the rock, pulling her, maybe, through the opening in the pond, back out to sea. And who could say what would happen then: if she would sink or float, or swim.

•

STANDING ON THE cliff, I see the grey-blue tail slice through the water again. The lava rock is cutting into my feet. There's a voice in my head that says *swim*. The shoreline is a face of sharp rock, there's no way out once you enter. But the voice calling to me is louder than Andrew, who is saying my name over and over. This time, I don't tell him to look. I point out to the uncommon wave, to the tail that keeps rising. I close my eyes, and I jump.

WAYFINDING
(air)

All that you touch you Change.
All that you Change, Changes you.
The only lasting truth is Change.

—Octavia E. Butler, *Parable of the Sower*

FLOCK MEMORY

Meanwhile, the wild geese, high up in that clean blue air, are heading home again.

—Mary Oliver, "Wild Geese"

GROWING UP, I kept my distance from Canada geese. Some kid told they me could break my femur with their beaks, and that was *it* for me. We were on a field trip to the Toronto Islands that day and the geese were everywhere, in flocks by the dozens. They would never get out of your way, no matter how fast you ran toward them. The ground was covered in their small pellet droppings: every spring and summer, in every park in the city. As girls, we had to say *ew-ew-ew*, as we ran from the pellets, as our classmates watched and laughed. I played along, but I didn't really think it was gross. The small pellets looked just like earth. And that's what they were: earth digested; earth returned. *Ew-ew-ew*: ecosystem, species system, fertilizer. Those geese weren't great for the lake, but they were the reason the grass came back each spring.

We went to the island often in spring and summer, because my mother's best friend lived in a small cottage-style house there. We didn't have enough money to leave the city, but we could afford the two-dollar ferry across the lake. The summer crowds on the island were endless though, and they did a number on the flocks: sliding their bread into the ecosystem, domesticating the geese for a season. They treated them like one of the attractions, like the small Ferris wheel they went there to ride. Watching all that commotion, my fear of the geese grew. But the truth was, I loved them in equal measure. Or rather, I loved to see them leave: the moment they'd unfold their black wings, honk, and rise over the lake to join one another. In fall, when the air was cold enough to feel it on your lips, to taste it, and you had to wear a second sweater; in October when you could watch their V move against the half-light of dusk, heading toward a perpetual summer—I loved them for that.

I wasn't a happy child. It moved me to watch them take off, the way a road trip did: like we might go on, like there might be a path—a current, a sky—that went on forever, that meant we didn't have to return to our life, our house, our feelings, or at least not for a very long time. I pointed to the sky when I watched them go, and felt awe in my chest with an equal measure of longing. I wanted to leave, to run away from home—alone if I had to. But geese don't do it alone. That's the first lesson of migration they teach you in grade school: for the flock to cross long distances, they need to work together.

Geese take turns at the crown of the V—guiding, creating uplift for the birds behind them. When a leader is tired, they simply drop back and rest on the air currents of others. A new bird shifts into place, over and over. Flocks can travel two thousand kilometres in a day this way, never losing sight of each other. Migrating in a V, they can communicate, and will always see if a member of the flock drops away. No bird ever lands alone. One or two will break away and glide with an injured goose to the earth. And they will remain together until their flock-mate recovers or passes away.

Geese mate for life. They are deeply bonded and will grieve a partner or a lost gosling for years; they'll hang their heads to show their grief, even stop eating. This is why they are sometimes aggressive: they're just protecting their families, keeping us away from their nests, which are often in city parks or on golf courses. They also pass migration patterns down through generations; they carry memory between them as a flock. So maybe the species remembers, too, that something isn't quite right in our relationship. Maybe they know, in a way beyond words, how close they came to extinction at our hands. How close they came to flying on, past the horizon line, past summer, into a world beyond numbers, beyond records, beyond life.

THAT'S HOW IT seemed, as I got older: like the geese might just fly off forever. I knew they were a protected species—nearly extinct, not so long ago—and fewer returned to my neighbourhood each year. There was less shit in the park, and less grass growing, too, just a lot more mud that would cover your sneakers as soon as you bought new ones. The weather was changing, as well. It was easy to mark it because I was born on the second of May, and I could measure the change by what I wore each year, and where I sat crying. I was always crying on my birthday. Sometimes in a park, in a dress. Sometimes in a park, in a thrift-store winter jacket. I was a sad kid. *Emotionally sensitive.* And my birthday always seemed like a good opportunity to contemplate loneliness, and the fact that it would go on forever.

There was always birdsong at that time of year, even when the snow was still piled into hard, yellow clumps at the side of the road. I knew where to find the chickadees in the thin branches in the ravine, and sometimes a cardinal, lipstick-red. They lived there through the winter, and just got louder with dawning spring. But that *honk-honk,* on and on into a cacophony of honks—I stopped hearing it nearby, stopped worrying about their shit and my teenage sneakers. I lived far from the lake, that much was true, but that hadn't stopped them in my childhood. They'd still shown up on the field, running across the schoolyard before opening their wings and rising together. Landing there again in spring. And I'd understood, in some quiet way, that I was born in goose season, that I was born when their migration returned. In a line of birthdays marked by absences, this was just one more. *You grow up, you lose things*—that's what the world was telling me. And I figured maybe this meant *everything.* Maybe you just had to get used to disappearance. Your sense of awe, the people in your life, the birds. Someday, the world.

The truth is, I almost disappeared, too. I wanted what the migratory birds had: a flock, a flight plan, a chance to leave my life—at least for a season. But I was too young for a driver's licence, a car, a plane ticket, a credit card. What I had was a ticket to an all-night rave, temporary wings, and the uplift of addiction.

"In the real world," Dr. Gabor Maté wrote in *The Realm of*

Hungry Ghosts, reflecting on addiction, "there is no nature vs. nurture argument. Only an infinitely complex and moment-by-moment interaction between genetic and environmental effects."

Some people say you are always an addict, the way birds are birds. But what I see in myself are flight patterns; I see myself seeking a good place to land, and a way to get there. What in us does not change, when our circumstances do—for the better, or worse? There are rattlesnakes that no longer rattle; there are hawks learning to fertilize their own eggs. "Not why the addiction," Maté said, "but why the pain." Why the adaptation; why the absence of Canadian geese from my neighbourhood, when I turned fifteen.

IN MY FOURTH year of high school, I switched to my fourth school. It was at the edge of the water, right up against Lake Ontario. Only one hundred students were enrolled there, and the teachers went by their first names. You could watch the lake move outside the second-floor windows of the classrooms, and that's what I did, as I got mostly sober. I watched the lake, as my teachers spoke about globalization and Noam Chomsky, taught us to meditate and played guitar. I walked the paths nearby and smoked cigarettes, often not by myself anymore, because suddenly there were people around me, dressed in bright colours, their laughter echoing in the corridors. I let my hair grow out and started wearing brass jewellery from the Salvation Army. I felt a bit more alive. And the geese were there that year. They hadn't disappeared, they'd just found a new way to survive. The warmer weather, the golf courses, the city parks filled with bread and litter—they didn't need to migrate so much anymore. Flocks had moved into High Park and onto the island, full-time. And the others, the ones still flying south, they'd just changed their flight patterns. They didn't rest in the north end of the city anymore; they waited until they reached the harbour, where I'd also touched down. And then they floated in the lake together, buoyant, as we sat on the stones, eating lunch.

One day, I remember, I watched two goslings float behind their mother. Air cold in my mouth, a cigarette in my hand, the boys playing handball against the brick building. I stubbed out the red embers, and then saw the family of them rise, suddenly startled, straight from the water into flight. They didn't need land at all. They soared up, past the abandoned factory behind our school, an enormous heritage structure of rusted steel on the water's edge. They flew on, where the blue of the water met the blue of the sky, and then they were gone.

They'll be back, I thought—a new kind of thought—as I went into class. I bought a suede coat from the 1970s that fall. It had a collar of thick raccoon fur, and it only kept my neck warm. The rest of me was busy trying to be beautiful, and for the first time thinking I might succeed. At the beauty. At the sobriety. More geese flew over us, a new V each day. They rose high and higher, until only the neighbourhood flocks were left, and the gardens around us peeled back into twigs, and the trees could no longer hide groups of girls smoking joints, and we asked our teacher if we could meditate at the start of each class, and he always said yes even though we were avoiding our work, because the joke was really on us. I shared red lipsticks with my new best friend Emily. Flock memory. That's what I see, turning back toward that winter. Alit, afloat; I am not singular, anymore. By the lake, we turn our heads together: to west, to sunset. Someone turns on a CD in the student lounge, and we dance as one.

RARE HONEY

T'S EARLY WINTER when I meet with the bee-keepers from Hives for Humanity. There's been a cold snap and there's frost on the ground, which doesn't happen often in Vancouver. In their hives, the bees have slowed down and joined into a quivering mass with the queen at the centre, to make sure she's protected and warm. At least, that's the hope. It is difficult for the bees to make it through winter, and this cold snap will be hard for them. Many beekeepers open their hives in spring to find nothing. Sara Common rests her hand on a hive named Phoenix and tells me they will test the weight of the boxes midway through the season, to see if the bees are still there. For the past two winters, they've been lucky. Or maybe not *lucky*, exactly. They've worked hard to protect these hives, the way this community has worked hard to protect everything here—their housing, their safety, one another.

We're in the heart of the Downtown Eastside (DTES), what developers call *prime real estate*, what headlines call *ground zero* of the opioid epidemic, and what other people simply call *home*. This lot—58 Hastings—has been the site of two tent cities, and years of protesting and activism for housing rights.[1] Standing in the cold, it's hard not to step through a door of memory—the way trauma insists you do, sometimes—and see myself at fifteen. My context was very different from this one, though. The depth of the loss that opioids have caused here; the deep entanglement of colonialism and genocide within this context—these are things I will never truly comprehend. (For more on this, see The Understory: "On Survival," page 235.)

Gabor Maté was drawing from his experience working in the DTES when he wrote: "Addiction is not a choice anyone makes … it's not a moral failure; it's not an ethical lapse; it's not a weakness of character; it's not a failure of will."[2] And I think of his words as I pull myself back to the present—to Sara Common, smiling, her hand still resting on Phoenix. The lot was cleared and made ready for the garden, she's telling me, by a group calling themselves the *homeless soccer team*. I smile now, too, and shuffle my frozen feet. And I'm grateful to start walking again when she suggests we head to the other garden, where the project began.

YOU CAN TASTE an apiary distinctly, it turns out, by the flowers the bees have pollinated. Clover or buckwheat, wildflowers or cherries. But in the city, it's never a single crop you are tasting. Each neighbourhood has its own combination of blossoms, trees, life. And that's what you can taste, steeped in the comb: the complexity of life growing there.

This morning, before Sara brought me to the garden at 58 Hastings, we met up with her mother, Julia Common, at a café a few blocks away. "You can actually line up the honeys from the neighbourhoods and always know the Hastings honey," Julia told me, as I mixed a spoonful into my tea. "You can taste it. There's a certain flavour that hits you as you get closer to the *heart*."

By the *heart*, she meant Elizabeth, the first hive they set up in 2012, in the small garden beside Insite, farther up on Hastings. Established in 2003, Insite was the first legal safe injection site for IV drug users in North America. It has continued to operate under a constitutional exemption to the Controlled Drug and Substances Act—though keeping its doors open has required constant organizing, advocacy, and bringing forth challenges to the Supreme Court of B.C. and Canada.[3]

"Sara had been working on the Eastside for many years, and it scared me," Julia said, as I sat listening, scribbling notes. "I didn't understand it, I thought she was putting herself in danger for people who perhaps would not be loyal back to her. Those are my biases. Then I tried to be embracing, come down and have coffee with her and stuff like that, but two Aprils ago, she said: 'You know, that's great, but I wonder if we could do something meaningful together? What about bringing one hive down to the Eastside?' For me that was a huge stretch. But that's how we started. She had the vision, I had the bee knowledge."

They didn't expect the first hive to produce honey; they simply wanted to share the experience of beekeeping with the neighbourhood. But Elizabeth created forty litres of honey its first summer, twice the amount of Julia's hives on pristine farmland near Tsawwassen. In rural settings, there's no way to protect the bees from what's happening on neighbouring farms. The three biggest threats are almost always present: GMO plants that can be difficult for the insects to process; monoculture crops that offer only a limited period for pollination; and the use of neonicotinoid insecticides. These days, bees can often survive better in the city than the countryside.

Sara started to add a few more words, about the benefits of getting hands in soil, but then we both paused, realizing her mother was wiping her face, trying to hide how emotional she had become.

"Sorry, I can't help it." Julia shook her head, and looked back at her daughter for a moment. "I'm just such a doofus," she went on. "I didn't want to be down here. Then in the middle of the first summer, we'd just had our first taste of honey. Jim, a volunteer, is looking at the bees and he says, 'Next year, could we make two out of this one?' Of course, he's completely spot-on. That's what you do. I ask my daughter, 'Does anyone talk about the future down here? Because I'm talking to Jim about spring.'"

I AM STILL thinking about Julia's words, when we reach the Hastings Folk Garden beside Insite. Jim meets Sara and I there. He's wearing a thin denim jacket, obviously handling the cold better than I am. It's a small garden; the lot is the size of a house or so. There's nothing blooming in December, but there's still plenty to see: in the south corner, a women's bench with a dedicated plaque and memorials, and at the north end, the wood frame of a sweat lodge.

"A lot of people are trapped within these three blocks," Jim tells me. "This is the only green space. Respect for it is high."

He moves and speaks gently as he shows me around, speaking about the moods of the bees, how they recognize the keepers by their scent. He points out where they project movies in the summer against the brick wall of Insite, then finally brings me to the west wall, to Elizabeth, the heart of the network. The hive is unremarkable, a hand-painted box on a stand. But inside, Jim reminds me, sixty thousand bees should be vibrating slowly, protecting one another, as they wait for spring.

LATER, I SIT in the Drug User's Resource Centre, also known as *Lifeskills,* with Ian Smyth—another Hives for Humanity beekeeper. "You know, humans are the most resilient of all creatures," he tells me. "There's no difference between someone living on the street to someone living in a home. It's survival. The guy who lives on the street may become a little harder because he always has to be on his guard. We adapt, just like the bees adapt."

Ian lives in one of the single-room occupancy suites operated by the Portland Hotel Society. A notice about the bees was slipped under his door, and that's how he got involved. Now he's the main caretaker of five hives. "It gives me the sense that I'm actually protecting humanity by protecting the bees," he says quietly, and shrugs. "I'm making sure that there's going to be food and pollination. A little strange, but it means a lot to me. It's hard to explain the feeling you get, observing what's going on in the hive, realizing the bees communicate through dance, completely in the dark. It's awe inspiring. Most people think insects do everything by instinct, but I've seen bees actually problem-solve. How can you say that they're not thinking? We need to rethink what we consider intelligence to be. They have a brain, they have moods. They have the same bad days that we do as humans."

As the room moves around us, filling with loud conversations and laughter, people taking shelter from the cold and doing laundry in the community machines, Ian shifts in his seat and admits he's not the most social person. "I'm not involved in the alcohol or anything, so I didn't really have a reason to go outside. But the bees forced me to go out into the community. Now people see me around and say, 'There goes the bee guy.' I mean, how much alone time does a person really want in their life?"

I nod and laugh gently with him, because I can relate. "Our back deck used to be nothing but people throwing garbage out there," he adds. "Now we've got a garden. People that normally wouldn't say anything to each other are out there together all summer long."

It sounds like Ian is reciting poetry when he describes the bees: how they communicate a source of pollen, its distance and quantity, through a dance performed completely in the dark, how they trust and follow one another, constantly working to a greater purpose. I begin to lose myself in a vision: the community centre transforming into an intricate honeycomb, a hive that hums as each person performs their task. A social worker whistles as he passes, a couple shares noodles from a Styrofoam container while smiling deeply at each other, the dryer tosses sleeping bags, two men laugh. Then Ian looks up at me, the expression on his face changing. "If the human race were structured more like bees, you'd never have a problem in your life knowing where you're supposed to be. As soon as they emerge from their cell, they've got a job to do. If humans were born that way, having everything they needed …" And the vision, delicate as it was, fades.

We walk to the door together, and I ask if he thinks things in the neighbourhood will change. "If you ask me," Ian says, "it's changing for the worse. People in these condos are complaining about poor people. Well, you moved into this neighbourhood. What do you think you're going to do? Just sweep us under the rug and we won't exist anymore? Come on. The more they squeeze, the more people will get together and start fighting back. Not violently, but by any means possible. Maybe there'll be a revolution coming."

"With the bees?" I ask him, smiling.

"No, with the people," he responds. And then laughing, we speak over each other: "With the bees and the people," we say.

LATER THAT NIGHT, I eat the Hastings honey with a teaspoon, letting a mouthful slowly dissolve. The flavour is deep and unexpected. "Complex," Ian called it. There's no way to separate it from Ian's voice now, from the small, painted hives I saw in the gardens. I remember the words of Dr. Vandana Shiva, whose activism focuses on our rights to seeds: "The beauty of the seed is out of one you can get millions. The beauty of the pollinator is that it does that work of turning that one into a million. And that's an economics of abundance, of renewability, an economics of mutuality. That's to me the real economics of growth. Because life means growth and abundance."[4]

The beauty of the pollinator is the beauty of the beekeeper, I think. And this rare honey, maybe it's the taste of life growing, wherever and however it can.

THE FAILSAFE

One drop of water hath no power, one spark of fire is not strong, but the gathering together of waters called Seas, and the communion of many flames do make both raging and invincible elements. And una Apis, nulla Apis, one Bee is no Bee, but a multitude, a swarm of Bees uniting their forces together, is very profitable, very comfortable, very terrible, profitable to their owners, comfortable to themselves, terrible to their enemies.

—Samuel Purchas, *A Theatre of Politicall Flying-Insects,* 1657

I. The Bee Dancer

SITTING ON MY pink couch, alone in my one-bedroom apartment, I watch a woman dance, cloaked in bees, in a video on YouTube. The artist calls herself *Bee Dancer*. She looks straight at the camera, in the spring-bright field, surrounded by a swarm.

As the lens pulls to a wider focus, you see her entire body. Her torso is covered in twelve thousand bees, swarming and latched onto her skin. They cover her naked chest in a thick blanket, her breasts, her neck, her shoulders a moving cloak of bees. She moves her hands slowly, rhythmically, in what she calls *contemporary performance*. She leans back, toward the woods behind her, her bee neck leaning toward the sky. You can see her top lip swollen and red already, stung multiple times. Still, she moves in near stillness, hypnotic, no longer seeming human. Two pink flowers in her hair, as if she's willed herself into a plant, a branch, a non-human entity for the swarm to land on.

When the camera spans behind her, it reveals her bare, hard-muscled back, half-cloaked in bees near the shoulder. And that's when I see, for the first time, the piece of metal wire tied around her neck. I follow the line of the wire as she turns again, and finally see the square-shaped box that lies on her chest beneath the mass of bees. Which means the YouTube comments are true: the dancer is wearing a queen bee, trapped in a cage around her neck.

I would be angry at her, but I think I get it—I'm a storyteller, too. The bees come for you, and you go to them, and it's not simple how we meet. If the artist wanted to create something you couldn't look away from; if she wanted to remind the world of the places where we touch, she did that five million times, five million views over.

The place where we meet the bees: it is alive, thrumming, constantly changing. It is an intersection of risk and endangerment, where the survival of our bodies collide over and over, and most of the time there is a queen being placed in a cage.

At any given moment, thousands of caged queens are in cardboard boxes in the mail. Intercontinental mail, national mail. Those boxes are in the carriages of planes, in offices, in P.O. boxes and small trucks, heading toward new ecosystems, to foreign homes to repopulate, to form new broods, and mass honey. This is done to regain some of what we've lost, protect what can still be protected, and maintain the fragile food system we have built. And it is the largest migration in the world.

The artist was doing what hobbyists, children at agricultural fairs, and frat guys have done for decades. What she calls contemporary performance, others call *bee beards,* and they are all over YouTube. The behaviour of honeybees is predictable; predictable enough to place a caged queen around the neck of a child, or guy who has had too many beers, as long as he can stay still. Honeybees will always follow a queen to the place where she lands—or the place where we put her—and gather around her, moving slowly in a gathering mass of protection and warmth. Outside their hive, no longer guarding their territory and resources, they are in their calmest state. They are in their natural state of reproduction, regeneration, and your body is just a temporary stay. Wherever the queen goes next, the bees will follow. To a new location the scouts find, if left to their own devices—the inside of a tree, maybe, where they will begin to build new comb, hanging from the wood. To a new location where you place her, if you are completing a split. Or if the extraction has been done for show, for art, for laughs, they'll return with the queen to her hive. Exhausted, depleted, but soon ready to take up their tasks again. Their assigned, perfected roles, that make the colony what it is: a being that is never quite divided, a being whose parts cannot really be understood as separate from the whole.

II. One Bee Is No Bee

UNA APIS, NULLA *apis.* One bee is no bee. *Apis mellifera,* the European honeybee, is a *eusocial* species, one of the rarest types of social structures and the most cooperative there is. For some eusocial species—like the honeybee—this means that even the biological function of a creature can be adapted to serve the needs of its community; including sex, reproduction, and genetic composition. For example, to create a queen, workers choose to feed a single larva more. As a result it sexes, transforms, and becomes the sole reproducer in the hive. Likewise, when the hives decide it's time to re-create, reproduce, swarm, the workers begin feeding the active queen less, so she can soar. All of this is communicated by scent, by hormones, by instincts we don't fully understand. For all our observation—labs, studies, and centuries—until very recently, we believed a queen could only be formed by being fed royal jelly. But royal jelly is given to all bee young. It's the proportion that counts, in forming the queen.

Couldn't we have guessed this, after centuries? Proportion is everything in the hive. In *On the Origin of Species,* Charles Darwin observed: "We hear from mathematicians that bees have practically solved a recondite problem, and have made their cells of the proper shape to hold the greatest possible amount of honey, with the least possible consumption of precious wax in their construction."[1]

The hexagons bees create are geometrically precise: six equal line segments; six equal angles. And it's overcrowding that sets a hive toward splitting and swarming; when the bees perceive the population is no longer proportional to the size of their hive, they ready their queen for flight.

The names we have given the bees suggest hierarchy, delineation, rule: the queen at the top, with reigning power. But is that structure present at all? Or like the theory of royal jelly, are we simply observing ourselves? For one thing, the *observation effect:* the act of observation always changes what is being observed. And for another, the overwhelming evidence of our bias: attribution bias, confirmation bias, selection bias, gender bias.

Queen, colony, worker, drone—these words belong to our constructed power, not nature. For a long time, I thought this language must be a miscalculation, or misattribution; but really, it is a map of our relationship with the species—a map of the Anthropocene.

III. By Any Other Name ...

"THE PROGENY OF the *King*-bees is rather red," Aristotle reported, in *The History of Animals*, in 350 BCE. Seeing power and singularity, the biggest bee was gendered male by classical philosophy, and this idea carried on to the time of Shakespeare. From *King Henry V*: "So work the honey-bees; Creatures that, by a rule in nature, teach the art of order to a peopled kingdom. They have a king, and officers of sorts ..."[2]

And yes, *gender is a construct*—that exactly. A construct, a mechanism to speak and shape power, and you can watch its use change according to political rule. Shortly after the death of Queen Elizabeth, Charles Butler published *The Feminine Monarchie, or a Treatise Concerning Bees* in 1609, detailing the reproductive habits of honeybees. *Solertia et laboure*, it says on the opening diagram of the hive: *skill and industry.* In the years that followed, European industry began to refer to the *king* bee as the *queen* bee.

This shift in language also happened just as British settler colonialism was expanding. Soon after the *king* bee became the *queen*, colonies of European honeybees were shipped to what England called "the colonies," arriving in the Colony of Virginia by 1622. So, this language comes directly from source, and it exists as an intact record of violence, extractive views on labour, conquest, land, and force.[3]

In Europe in the 1600s, bees were used as core tenants of industry: sugar, booze, and electricity—honey, mead, and candles. Honeybees were brought over to sustain settlers, and allow for the cultivation of agriculture and industry, during the initial project of invasion, expansion, and occupation. These invasive species of bees swarmed, split their hives in the wild, reproduced and spread themselves through the woods, migrating through new ecosystems, as settlers followed just behind. There is a close historical relationship between the westward expansion of the colonial project, and western expansion of invasive hives. So they carry the very specific mark of their name: queen to Queen Elizabeth, colony to colonialism.[4]

LIKE GEMSTONES AND healing crystals, honeybees have often been seen as a symbol, an indicator, a metaphor, a mirror. I understood them like this for years, in a way that felt meaningful. *We are connected,* the honeybees told me. *God Save the Queen,* some T-shirts and posters read, with illustrations of bees—and I thought that was clever, even if I wanted the real monarchy erased from the structures of the earth. I thought the history of one tagline differed from the classic moniker. Environmentalism, colonialism—the same rhetorical core?

God save the record, *God save* the linguistics of invasion, *God save* Queen Elizabeth: it turns out that's exactly what they were saying. And I almost bought the T-shirt.

IV. The Keystone Is Mutual

WHAT WOLVES ARE to a forest, what prairie dogs are to an open plain, pollinators are to orchards, farms and wildflower fields. Specifically, pollinators are *keystone mutualists*—a type of keystone species that relies on a bonded, mutual relationship to create a symbiotic, trophic cascade. Wild pollinators often exist in specific relationship to only one particular plant or flower. Butterfly Milkweed, for example, is the only food of monarch caterpillars. Evening primrose is the only food of the evening primrose sweet bee. The way geese mate for life, pollinators mate with plants; except their bond goes on for eternity—*till death do us part*—with the death of one genetic line often spelling the death of the other. Monarchs and milkweed: *star-crossed lovers*.

Apis mellifera interrupts this symbiosis because it outcompetes. Unlike specialized, endemic pollinators, European honeybees are generalist pollinators, widespread foragers, who can make it work with pretty much anyone: the milkweed, the primrose, the apple, the lavender, the almond flower. They will forage endemic plants that are the sole source of food for wild pollinators—leaving the wild species without the resources they need.[5] They will gather, basically, whatever exists in a field. Any speck of pollen, but also any speck of poison—any residue of pesticides that remains from the past decade. Their generality is why they can produce so much honey, why they are used for agricultural pollination, and it is also why we are in so much trouble.

We've built a colonial, agricultural empire on the back of a single invasive pollinator, who is highly sensitive to chemicals and dying all the time. The more we rely on them, the more we may reduce the diversity of wild pollinators—who now face not only endangerment, but extinction—which makes the cultivation of honeybees all the more crucial. And the fewer wild pollinators there are, the more we have to rely on domesticated ones—which leaves us in a vulnerable cycle. As if we've built a house of petals that could just blow away; except it's our entire food system.

INSECTS ARE RESILIENT, entomologists remind us. The survival of insects is critical, deeply entangled with our own, and in some ways, simple. One basic conclusion of the research seems to be that we are not the only creatures in our food system that need food. If there's enough forage—enough diverse, unpoisoned forage—there will be less competition, and in turn more pollination, more survival, more forage and food for us all. We'll all have more of a fighting chance. When insects are not starving, they are more resilient to pesticides, to disease, to invasive species. Insect habitats can be tiny, and have trophic effects; a single, endemic wildflower field makes a difference.

And yet: Bayer, the almond lobby; their intimacy with the USDA. What a mess, what a meta mess we've made out of things.

What's in a name?

An entire epoch.

V. Bees, aka *Livestock*

ACCORDING TO THE United States Department of Agriculture (USDA), honeybees are livestock. They are the only insect listed this way; the same as cattle or poultry. But they are at the heart of our food systems—they shape every third bite of food we take, some estimate—so how else would they be seen, by the USDA? By numbers, honeybees are estimated to be the basis of six hundred billion dollars worth of global food production each year. By numbers, 30–50 percent of the honeybee hives in the United States are dying each year. By numbers, cultivated honeybees are the only pollinators we count.[6]

The insect world is diffuse, varied, mostly unseen, highly incalculable: there are over one million known insect species, and they constitute more biomass, higher quantities, and more diversity than the entirety of animal life. Less than 1 percent of invertebrates have been assessed globally, but all studied were found in steep decline; more than 40 percent were considered threatened.[7] When this world dies, it falls right into the earth, it composts in the understory quickly. It leaves hardly a trace. So, we have to take some of our guesses from silence, from our clean windshields that used to be covered in bugs, from what we know of glyphosate, *Roundup,* and commercial bees collapsing.

Commercial bees aren't going extinct, many people point out. We won't let them. There are more honeybees than people in the United States right now. But the genetics of the bees are narrowing and narrowing; their ability to live without us is already mostly gone. They are not *endangered*, but they are constantly *in danger*, which means our food systems are in danger, and we are, too. Their numbers split even, because we split hives: hive after hive after hive, manufacturing birth as we do death as we do honey. Almost half the population is lost and remade each year. This is a drastic rise from decades past, where beekeepers expected around 5–10 percent losses.[8] And we can't really say how long that strategy will work, how long it can sustain itself, because for all our theories of control and domestication, for all the billions of bees in captivity—until recently, we still couldn't determine how hives made their queens.

In the midst of these unknowns, honeybees continue to be seen as an indicator species, as canaries in the coal mine, as the storytellers, even, of the fields. Because they are widespread foragers, because we count and watch them, they tell us what's happening beyond our eyes. Where they thrive, an ecosystem is thriving. Where they die, others are dying, too. They touch the invisible world with their antennae, with their lives, and return to their hives with a dance—a waggle dance, it's called, *how cute*—that reflects proximity and abundance of food nearby. But now, often their dance is simply their death, that speaks through its stillness of the proximity of pesticides nearby.

"An acute kill," one beekeeper called it, in the documentary *The Pollinators*. He was standing in an almond field in California, being interviewed as his hives fell around him. He lifted up his hand and all of the bees in it were still. And what we all know, what we can all sort out, is that *insecticide* is two words joined together, and one of them is *insect* and the other is *cide*, Latin for *kill*.

Pesticide, insecticide, neonicotinoids, *Roundup*. By numbers, we only know what we know. By numbers, "Death has sucked the honey from your breath," Romeo says to Juliet, when he realizes what they've done. "Come, bitter poison, come."

VI. Love in the Time of Glyphosate

IF HONEYBEES ARE storytellers, I return to the stories between us: drama, romance, classic tragedy. From the opening line of Gabriel García Márquez's *Love in the Time of Cholera*: "The scent of bitter almonds always reminded him of the fate of unrequited love."

In that story, a man has taken his own life by gold cyanide, and what is left of the poison is the aroma of almonds. In this story, we are hopelessly in love, the almonds are our beloved, and the fate of our bond shall be the fate of us all. Ecosystems always reveal high drama, when they are torn apart.

The play goes like this: it takes five litres of water to produce a single almond, and almond trees are grown in the desert. It takes five litres of water per almond, and there is a drought, and a multi-billion-dollar industry on the line. There is a multi-billion-dollar industry on the line that requires expansive pollination by more than two million honeybee colonies every February; that is, nearly every commercial colony in the United States. It requires two million colonies, but nearly one million colonies die every year. By one million colonies, I mean upward of seventy-five billion bees. I mean, every remaining colony must be split and reborn through the god-hand of commercial beekeepers. Beekeepers, birthkeepers: seventy-five billion dead, seventy-five billion born.[9]

The *apis industrial complex*, I've heard this system called, from the idea of an *animal industrial complex*, from the idea of the *prison industrial complex*.[10] But I think of it as the *pollen industrial complex*, from the idea of a *pain industrial complex*, from the idea of the *pharmaceutical industrial complex*, which is like: where there is pain, where there is pollen, there is profit. *Valnero, ergo sum:* I *hurt*, therefore I am. I *wound*, therefore I am. I *injure*, therefore I am. I order new healthy queens from Australia, I requeen my hives, therefore I meet my quotas.

Do I blame the beekeepers? I don't blame those entangled in the harm of this system. In our current world, suicide rates among farmers are often higher then veterans.[11] If you listen to interviews with beekeepers, they'll tell you their options are the almond orchards or bust; bankruptcy or Northern California. Their costs are rising as the bees' death counts are rising, so their choices have narrowed: the almonds fields, or the almond fields. And if they give up, the entire agricultural system collapses. Collapses, fractures, breaks along the fault lines of class, race, and hunger. So, they don't give up. They drive enormous trucks, stacked with hives, across the country in the middle of the night. From the almond orchards in February, to the apples, to the peaches, to the rest; and then they enact Lazarus on the species, raising whole colonies from the few bees that remain. Like midwives, like god-hands, like tenders of us all.

In Márquez's novel, the symptoms of love are the same as the symptoms of cholera. In *Romeo and Juliet*, to love each other is to die together. In the almond industry, almonds are touted as the heart-healthy choice. And in the almond fields, billions of bees are having unprotected sex with flowers that carry neonicotinoids, with the parasites and viruses of each other. High drama; high yields: 80 percent of the world's almond supply comes from these fields, 10 percent of California's water goes to these fields, alongside 95 percent of the nation's bees.[12] By the numbers, *a plague upon both your houses.* By the numbers, *come, bitter poison, come.*

OUTLAW THE ALMOND, I want to tell the world. *Save yourself.* Maybe potato chips will be the snacks that save us in the end— potatoes can be pollinated by wind. But my Irish ancestors would have something to say about that; they'd remember what happens to a nation whose survival is deeply tied to a single colonial crop; to potatoes specifically, when that food fails. One-eighth of the population of Ireland died in the Potato Famine, in only five years. *A blight upon all our houses,* upon the monocropped future, upon the soy, and the canola, and the almond.

The love we have for almonds will always be unrequited; they can't love us, can't love our ecosystem back. And we can't love them without tragedy.

There has to be another way, I mutter in the grocery store, and I can hear my ancestors laughing back at me—my grandmother standing in the middle of her enormous urban garden, tending rabbits for their meat in her shed. My grandfather planting rows of carrots beside his mobile home, his freezer full of venison he hunted: *Of course there is, kid.*

VII. The Failsafe

Pahoa, Big Island of Hawaii, Summer 2014

STANDING IN A muggy rainforest, I watch a woman pull the top bar out of a hive. The air is thick and wet, mosquitos are biting every part of me, and the hum of the bees is loud enough to feel in my chest. The beekeeper, Jen, is wearing a pink tank top and a baseball hat, no bee suit. Her hands are covered in bees. They are crawling up her arms, flying around her face. "I used to wear gloves," she tells us, "but the bees couldn't recognize me. I got stung even more." And then she says that she's just been stung twice, as if the stings were just kisses.

There are ten of us standing together in the small clearing. The others are wearing bee veils, but there wasn't enough equipment, and my face is bare like Jen's. "If you're nervous," she told me, "just stand back. The bees will sense it." But I don't want to stand back, now that we are here. I want my hands to be as steady as hers, under the moving feet of five thousand bees. I am standing beside a mass of them in motion; about to see one hive become two—about to see the hive give birth, basically. *Stay calm*, I tell myself as I step toward the open hive.

These bees are part of a permaculture project, run by a friend of mine, in an effort to grow more food on the property. A large community lives here; over a hundred people, a mix of guests on retreat, and long-term volunteers like me. The volunteers live in large tents at the edge of the jungle, and mine is just down the path from where we are standing.

Mostly, my presence on the island is a problem, a paradox. Tourists, foreigners, settlers, we can act like fire ants, like coqui frogs, like invasive species on the economic, cultural, and spiritual systems of the island. This is an island, after all, that was illegally annexed by the United States; part of an archipelago and sovereign kingdom that continues to face occupation.[13] Mostly, my American friends call this *America*. Mostly, we get things wrong. All night, you hear the music of the coqui frogs, and it sounds beautiful, maybe, like a chorus of crickets, but it also sounds like we've broken into the silence. For now, at least. There's no saying what the future of these ecosystems, these food systems—and even that silence—will be.

Native pollinators in Hawaii are in deep, deep trouble, experts keep saying—and so is the island's food security. Approximately 85 percent of food on the island is imported and this supply chain is increasingly at risk, in the face of extreme weather and supply chain problems. Producing domestically grown food is considered essential, difficult, and highly dependent on honeybees. The state department reports 70 percent of local food relies on cultivated hives.[14] Food sovereignty, food security; they are all tied up in protecting a species that both disrupts and preserves these biomes. The honeybees are a significant problem, but also may become a singular solution. Not a keystone, as much as a failsafe.

So that's what I'm watching, in motion. A failsafe on Jen's arms, covering her hands, rising in the air between us. The bees are flying around all of us now, half drunk on the herb smoke that was piped into their hives. Jen sweeps the bees from the wax, to show us where hexagons have been filled with a dark red substance: bee bread, royal jelly. She points at the irregular part of the hive— relatively large wax globes that the bees are forming at the edges, to create their future reproducer. "When you see these," she tells us, "you know the hive is ready to split."

Jen continues to lift the frames, one by one, looking for the queen. She isn't going to cage the matriarch. Jen practices biodynamic beekeeping. She doesn't use any chemicals in her hives. She is looking for a different way to do things: swarming, and splitting, and managing Varroa mites—a widespread parasite that infests hives, considered one of the leading causes of honeybee death. It's controversial, what she's doing. If you don't treat the mites, maybe their infection flourishes, maybe the bees carry those mites to colonies nearby, or worse, native pollinators.

Maybe the hives simply die, one by one, as you watch them. One by one, or all at once: a dozen, two dozen in a day. But if you do treat them, often the hives weaken over time. There is a genetic impact, even if they survive.

So, there's something else Jen is doing; there's something else I'm watching move, and split, and grow around us. The way farmers save heirloom seeds, Jen is attempting to preserve genetic lines of bees. Lines that know how to swarm, how to reproduce on their own; lines predisposed to survival in adverse conditions. These are *failsafes* of the *failsafe*. Where these lines survive, wild genes are maintained, tended like non-GMO seeds for the future.

IT'S HARD TO say what that future will look like. A few years from now, a volcanic fissure will split just down the road, and lava will pour through this neighbourhood. My aunt's house in Kapoho will get covered, completely erased by the flow. The main road to the retreat centre will be blocked by a huge wall of obsidian, and the retreat will shut down, maybe forever. There will be only one road left out of this place. Nature isn't passive. The fossil record laughs at the idea of human dominance, even if it looks that way sometimes. Land reclaims itself, eventually. Land reclaims itself, tectonically. And settler culture—my culture—is the only culture that seems to have ignored this truth throughout history.

VIII. The Golden Ratio

INSECTS ARE RESILIENT, entomologists say. Some more than others; cockroaches, say, or termites—those that work with erosion, disease, or death. Mutualism is everywhere, not just in life.

We need multiplicity and range for an ecosystem to function: bee and wasp, termite and moth, carrion and creation. And maybe, for our food system to survive: both keystone pollinators and failsafe bees.

Proportion is everything in a hive, as in nature. Proportion, proximity. With enough space, enough forage, these species don't have to compete. How devastatingly simple. *Plant some goddamn wildflowers*, I hear the canola field scream. *Set my milkweed free— or I will, by any means.* And then, as drought stretches out, and more insects are forced into proximity, that field reminds us: *just look what happens when you place two of my grasshoppers together.*

If two grasshoppers are forced into proximity—by drought, by habitat destruction—their pheromones kick in. They metamorphosize, transform into locusts, and eventually gather into a swarm. Not a swarm of reproduction, a swarm like the bees; this is a swarm of subtraction, dissolution, a gathering of biblical famine. On their own, grasshoppers can act as pollinators, but together, their collective noun is *plague.*

Proportion, proximity: they are everything.

King bee, queen bee, colony, we've called honeybees. Six hundred billion dollars a year, we've called them—as if life itself can be measured by GDP. If these bees, if these hives, have a number, I think it's 1.618—the golden ratio, found throughout nature, when nature expands. Seed heads, pine cones, nautilus shells— they all express this ratio, this sequence as they grow. The number of petals on a flower, the angles of a chicken egg, the branches on an oak tree, and the reproductive pattern of honeybees: all 1.618. Even under pressure, under collapse, honeybees continue to create family trees that follow these numbers. And this is who they really are, I think, when you strip away the language, the history of harm we've bound to them. They are a sequence, a golden mean, an equation of careful alignment, interspecies symmetry. Not hierarchy, but patterning; not rule but relationship. We've mucked it up, we've intervened and invaded, but this pattern remains, hoping to articulate itself in good relationship—pointing us toward a math of coexistence. And how could I not fall in love with that? With what it says about belonging, about survival. Nature wants to find a way. Nature is designed for coexistence. Nature is us; beyond the ways we have storied ourselves apart: a fertile human uterus still approximates the golden ratio, still acts like any seed head, any shell, any honeybee. And I find hope in that, if nowhere else. Hope, and grief, and persistence.

Save the bees, we say and yes, often we mean honeybees, and yes, maybe we really mean humanity. But isn't that worthy? Deeply worthy. To save the web, the comb, the connection between us. To save what we can—what we need—of our food systems. Save the bees; save the failsafe. Protect us all from famine. *May you never hunger,* we say as a blessing in my tradition. *May you never thirst.* And I mean it, with all that I am. I mean it, when I say *save the bees.*

WILDFLOWERS
(spirit)

But because truly being here is so much;
because everything here apparently needs us,
this fleeting world, which in some strange way
keeps calling to us. Us, the most fleeting of all.
Once for each thing. Just once; no more. And we too,
just once. And never again. But to have been
this once, completely, even if only once:
to have been at one with the earth, seems beyond undoing.

—Rainer Maria Rilke, "The Ninth Duino Elegy,"
translated by Stephen Mitchell

THE CUSTOM OF KILLING RABBITS

A letter to my grandmother after her death

Sharpen your knife,
break its neck quickly.
Skin the pelt and keep
the left foot for luck.
There is more than
one way to kill a rabbit,
but this was your way:
do not lose any meat,
do not tear any fur.
Stuff with thyme and blacken.
Eat with zucchini flowers,
dripping hot oil.

Y OU SLAUGHTERED YOUR rabbits each
spring. I remember holding them, small
and alive in our hands, their hearts beating
like wings. We'd stand in your shed, in your backyard, delighted,
unaware what would happen next. Young as we were, we knew
little about the customs you'd carried here, and less about the gift
of tending your own meat. When you served us dinner, your life
was part of the life you offered, wasn't it? You understood what
sacrifice meant.

I remember standing in your backyard in a bone-white dress,
with a choker of red plastic beads. You held the screen door open,
and an orange cat wandered out of the house, slipped between
the high, green tomato stalks. My sister laughed beside me, her
hair full of curls. Sunlight fell onto everything, and no one spoke.
We picked handfuls of yellow flowers from the zucchini for you
to batter and fry. That summer, you were filled with laughter. Your
skin dark, glowing with sun. You poured olive oil into your palms
and spread it across your thick arms, your face, speaking loudly in
a language I could not understand.

I remember standing beside you at the stove. You were fat,
beautiful, larger than life. There was tomato sauce cooking in a
cast-iron pan, and you gave me a piece of white bread to dip in it.
I ate beside you, shy and hungry. I didn't realize the meat came
from the rabbits, yet. There were pots on every burner, water boil-
ing, mason jars clinking as they were heated and sealed. Those
jars filled with skinned tomatoes, eggplants, mushrooms, and
fava beans. This was how you saved your garden through winter.
This is what we took home, each time we left: food that could last
my family until spring.

Each winter, I'd stare up at those jars, sitting on the high shelf in our family's apartment in Toronto, where the cupboards often looked bare. The mushrooms covered in oil and chili peppers, the eggplants skinned and cut into strips. I'd think of you. I'd think of Sault Saint Marie, and the Canadian Shield we crossed to get to you, of our long drive past rock walls that seemed like they would never end.

The autumn you died, there were still jars in your root cellar. Your sons divided them between our families, and we opened them with care: each mouthful a sacred act, our loss counted down in litres. You were there with us at Christmas, for the first time in years. Months after you'd crossed over, feeding us as we sat together by candlelight, drinking cheap red wine. "*Mangia*," your youngest son said, like you used to, as his wife took a roast rabbit from the oven and carved it, still steaming, for our plates.

You passed away in your sleep. As if swept by the hand of a gentle god into another room of belonging. An inhale, an exhale, then a dream that led into obliterating light. I can't think of a kinder way to go. Rabbits in the shed, your gold necklace on the dresser. That orange cat curled at your feet, as you went to meet the ferryman.

The moment you crossed over, I felt it. I woke suddenly, sat upright in bed, shivering, clutching the covers to my chest. I was filled with a sadness I could not understand. The moon shone bright over Montreal; it was three o'clock in the morning. I pulled my blankets around me and stood by the window, staring at the fluorescent cross on Mount Royal, full of grief. A thousand kilometres from your home, I watched you go into the night.

If you shook me awake to say goodbye, to press a kiss to each of my cheeks; if you stayed for a moment, standing beside me as I studied the glow of streetlights, a presence over my right shoulder: know that I heard you. You did not travel alone. Years before I understood what it meant, I felt you.

I couldn't name what had happened, so I turned away. A few days later, my father left for your funeral and I did not go with him. "It's fine," he said, "it doesn't matter." He was wrong, of course; confused by grief, likely. I stayed in Montreal for an arts festival I had organized, and he drove over the Canadian Shield, through all those miles of rock, without sleeping. He couldn't afford a motel. Gas station coffee and endless cigarettes, his one headlight shining through that cold October night; that's how I picture him. Maybe you were with him, guiding him, making sure he got to your bedside safe.

Your bed was already empty, of course. Everything was different, he said, and everything was the same. But the rabbits were still in the shed, he told me later. In fall, the garden was just a nest of dead stems, but they'd grow again in summer. You only planted perennials. What's the use of a plant that dies as soon as the frost sets in? You grew what could outlast even your body. I wish someone had thought to save those seeds.

Any distance I felt between us in life, fell away in death. The lack of closure, my absence at your funeral, created a holding pattern. The shame I felt for not being there; it kept me looking back, over my shoulder. And every time I did, I saw you standing there. I don't feel shame anymore. I feel you beside me nonna, like a gentle presence; one that guides me back and forth through time.

You kept traditions for your dead. After your husband died, I'm told you wore black for five years. Even in summer, you stood in your garden in a dark dress. This was the custom for women back home, mourning as a public act. These days, I am learning my own rites of grief, mixed with your customs. Last year, I cooked

my first rabbit. It was the end of October, when many traditions say you can hear your ancestors, if you listen. Halloween,
Samhain—Il Giorno dei Morti, they call it in Calabria—*Day of
the Dead*. All over the world, we've done similar things at this
threshold, where the fallow season begins: gathered, celebrated,
honoured the dead. In your village, ancestors hide gifts throughout the house in the middle of the night. Children wake joyfully
to toys and chocolate placed there by ghosts. Everyone gathers in
the cemetery, with candles and flowers, and laughter. And in the
evening, they feast.

These are your people, these rituals tell us—the good and the
bad, the dead and the living. You don't have to feed them all, but
it matters to know them, to learn virtue, caution, and repair from
what they've done. One day, you'll join them. One day, maybe,
you'll be honoured like this.

You are my people, nonna—you with your hands on the rabbits, you tending death for the sake of our food. In your village,
children laugh in the graveyards, like they laugh in the streets of
Pompeii. We reach over, we touch, and it is more than a haunting.
If we turn toward it, it's an offering.

When I planned to cook the rabbit, I asked my uncle for your
recipe. I drove to a neighbourhood where they sell hand-tended
meat. That rabbit lived well, I think, like yours did. It was skinned
and frozen, but still had its shape, its bones. I didn't look away
from what it was; I thought of its life, of your shed, as I said my
thanks.

My friends gathered in my kitchen that night. They laughed all
around me, drinking cheap wine. I lit candles, set a plate for you,
and cut fresh rosemary from the garden. Then I carved the rabbit,
still steaming. "*Mangia*," I told my friends. "Come eat."

THE STING

I.

WHEN THE BEE stings me in the heart, I'm entering a café on Commercial Drive. It's a warm and bright day, even though it's September. The windows of the café are open and everyone seems to be laughing, as they wait for the poetry reading to start. Everyone, including one of my exes—the one who ghosted me last spring—who is leaning on the bar, looking tanned and happy from touring their bike up the coast all summer. They shrug when they see me enter the room, shrug with their hands in their pockets and smile. And I smile back like I haven't begun to drift out of my body, helium-like, to avoid this.

"Hi," we both say, walking over. "Hi, so good to see you." Then we go in for a hug, and that's when it happens: the bee that has flown down my dress is pressed between us. The stinger barbs into my skin, seems to go right into my sternum.

"Fuck fuck fuck!" I shout against their body, jerking away, tearing at my dress.

"What what what?" they say, startled.

"A fucking bee," I say.

A wild bee. It falls from my dress to the sticky café floor, dying. They rush to the bar to get ice. The sting keeps rising, burning brighter. Shock, epinephrine: I can feel my body preparing for flight. They return with a pint glass of ice cubes, already melting in the heat. Look me right in the eyes, like time has turned back to spring. "Are you okay?" they ask.

The ice is cold in my hand, it sticks to my skin as I shove it down my dress, press it between my breasts. I hold it there, dripping wet, cold, and painful against the hot sting. I can still see the bee dying on the floor. Nature doesn't lie, but I do. "It's getting better already," I say.

II.

ALONE IN MY one-bedroom apartment in East Vancouver, I've been rolling organic tobacco and drinking enough coffee to stain my teeth. I've been setting time limits for when I can begin watching TV—5:00 p.m., *no*, 3:00 p.m.—and then breaking them. I've been considering how I dealt with isolation as a teenager, and my proximity to downtown. *Maybe I should get a cat*, I've been thinking, but it seems pretty clear I can't take care of anything; not the dishes long sitting in the sink, not the eroding soles of my cowboy boots, not my sublet apartment. I don't even have a lease. *Give me something,* I've been praying at life, *give me some way to go on.* And then the bee flies down my dress.

The stinger goes right into my heart, like a rapier, like a stiletto knife, like it is ten thousand times what it is. The ice drips down my dress, the bee is there on the floor, dying, and I have been so lonely. I have been so alone. I've been hiding it in these dresses, that's the art of femme: *you are so beautiful,* everyone says while you lie all night in a bathtub that could be the bottom of a river. The stinger, it goes so deep it's blood-deep, love-deep, "I'm totally fine," I say, and the ex walks away as the sting continues rising. Burning, rising. I lift the bee from the filthy floor. I carry it with me to the bathroom where I look into the mirror and study the place where our bodies have become one. I can't see the stinger, but I know it's in there, making its way into grief.

So you died for this? I ask, and silence answers. Elsewhere, the hive goes on, recreating itself. But here, this sacrifice says my name. It says my name only. *How special you are,* it tells me. *To be a body a bee can sting. To be living.*

I place the carapace in toilet paper, into my purse. I wash my hands. *To be living.* I wash my face. *To be living.* And it echoes, what the bee has told me. It echoes; it thrums, it doesn't stop burning. *1,* I hear when I'm falling asleep, *1, 2, 3.* And when I sit at my desk: *5, 8, 13, 21.* I hear the Fibonacci sequence, the metre of the golden ratio, and it's like synesthesia, like my senses mix: I hear the number, I see light, I see gold, I see wings. I write the number in lipstick on my mirror, the way other people write *I love you:* 1.618. "You aren't alone," I say to myself, to my reflection in my empty apartment, "you are part of everything."

III.

IN THE HOMEOPATHIC remedy, *apis mellifica*, a honeybee is crushed and added to alcohol. The mixture is then diluted with water, over and over, until something new is made: a medicine with trace amounts of bee venom that can be used to treat bee stings.

Like cures like, homeopathy says. A drop of the poison becomes the cure. The body responds to the trace, to the memory, to the molecule. And rather than fighting it, inflammation calms; not just on the site of the bite, but everywhere.

Dosis sola facit venenum—the dose makes the poison, homeopathy says. From Paracelsus (c. 1493–1541), the so-called father of toxicology: "What is there that is not poison? All things are poison and nothing is without poison. Solely the dose determines that a thing is not a poison."

What homeopathy does with bee venom, it does with snake venom, with poison ivy. Inside the ailment, you find the remedy, if you pay attention. *Turn toward it*, homeopathy suggests—just like my therapist—*don't look away*.

"How much alone time does a person really want?" I hear Ian say. Each body has its own dosage, its own threshold: for venom, for violence, for isolation and loss. At my tipping point, the bee stings me in the heart, and it calls me back, it raises me from the bottom of the muddy lake, the river. Within isolation: connection.

To be living, the sting says. It takes years, it burns for years like the stinger is still in me. The depression goes nowhere, but it is not mine alone. And eventually I'm standing in an apiary, in the rainforest; I'm standing in an apiary, in the Downtown Eastside;

I'm standing in a literal field, on the island I've moved to—the island where I was once bitten by a tick—and the bees are rising around me.

IV.

The bees come for you.

My friend Grace is a beekeeper. "They came for me," she tells me and lights her joint, on her farm with its open well and fig trees. And then, one year on her farm, they all die, the bees, hive after hive. "They came for me," I hear her say, and then I watch her stack the empty boxes, over and over again in my mind. The crates are painted pale blue, and she is crying. The figs fall to the ground and split. All the elders I know are becoming death doulas. The young people I know are becoming birth doulas. Grace, I think, is becoming both.

On Monday afternoons, when her daughters are away, I sit with Grace in her kitchen and we write together. She is writing a play where God opens her mouth at the moment of creation and a swarm of bees fly out. She gives me a jar of honey, from a year when the bees were alive, and I eat the honey slowly, I savour every spoonful, I make it last years.

"To create a single jar of honey," Grace tells me, "the bees need to travel the distance to the moon and back." To the moon and back, for a single jar of honey. A small jar, at that: ten ounces.

How far for this spoonful, then? I ask every time I open the mason jar she gave me, with its piece of intact comb. A few times, I've broken off a piece of that comb and sucked it until there was nothing left but wax. *How far for that? How many oceans?* A table-spoon is the distance, maybe, from Grace's kitchen on Salt Spring Island to where I grew up in Toronto.

This sacrifice says your name, the sting in my heart told me. And the honey? That ghost honey Grace gave me, from a hive that had already fallen to mites, to climate change: *I still love you*, it said. *I love you, I love you to the moon.*

V.

What do you call a beekeeper who has no bees?

A beekeeper.
The future.
Both.

Like a mother, like a widow, like a miscarriage: loss doesn't unmake who we are.

VI.

GRACE HASN'T BROUGHT hives onto her farm again. Her partner and daughters helped burn the old boxes; there's always a chance that fungus or mites have made it right into the wood. Like the winter my friends went to repair their farmhouse and found out the walls were all rotted through: they had to tear down half the house, with the rain coming down, just to save the good part of their home. You have to begin again. And to begin again you have to be ready to lose it all, to see the hives blacken and fall.

"I'll start again," she tells me, "when it's time." And then she puts on her costume—her play is written now—and she's the queen, the lost queen, she's the bee and she's the first mouth of creation, opening wide for the bees to fly out.

In her art, Grace becomes the ninety thousand bees that died in her garden that spring, and it's funny—side-splittingly funny—because Grace, it turns out, has been studying clowning, true *bouffant* for years, and so we get to laugh as we break into sobs. There's no stage. She performs on her farm where the bees are all gone, so you can cry right into the dirt, right into the open well that feeds a willow, right into her shoulder. And she'll stay with you when it's over, you won't be alone.

VII.

I love you, the hive says. *I love you to the moon.*

What do we say back?

Grace was arrested dressed as the queen bee, this summer. She was deep in the forest, at the Ada'itsx/Fairy Creek Watershed. In the photographs, you see her perched ten feet up, in some kind of rigged-up wooden contraption. At first she's just holding a red umbrella, up there in the rain, and you can tell she's in role, that's she's buzzing, she's smiling, and everyone below her must be laughing as well. *I love you*, she's telling the crowd, she's telling the forest. And then, the photos show a giant yellow excavator rise toward her. It's come to take her away. The shovel head goes so close to her, it's like she's earth, it's like she's dirt suspended, midair. And then: there's the RCMP, two large men on a ladder grabbing Grace, taking her from her perch to arrest her. And even though it's a photograph, you can see the moment they almost drop her, the moment they almost send her through the air, a women in her fifties, as if she really does have wings.

VIII.

HERE IS THE keystone: us. We are not alone. We reach out and something reaches back. That's it, simply: we exist together. And because of that, the bridge doesn't fall.

WILDFLOWERS

THE RADIO IS on, Tom Petty sings, and in this vision we lower the car windows, we let the summer roll onto our bare shoulders. We belong, like Tom Petty says, somewhere we feel free and we feel it. We feel it in our bare legs, feel it in the bag of gas station chips between us. At the end of where we are heading, there is a picnic blanket spread out in a field. There is sparkling water because we don't drink, and tarot cards and a river. A good clean river, where we can throw off our summer dresses and wade in. Lay ourselves down, gasping with the deep cold. Laughing as we see the shock in each other. We'll find the hard stones under our feet. We'll let our hair braid with the flowing water, and I'll think: *free, free, thank god I'm free.*

It's been the hardest of years. "As for the pain and suffering we have come through together," you said in your letter, "I've had enough." Into the envelope you'd placed wildflower seeds. "Plant these," you said, "let nature do its magic."

My friend: we will rise from that river, dripping that river, and dry ourselves in a field of wildflowers, someday. Just lie there, the way pollen does, waiting for the sun to make it right. When the bees come, when the ants drift over our skin, that's belonging.

I did not know I could love myself this way: like a shallow river, like a cornflower, like a seed that never breaks and is forevermore a seed.

This is the magic, right? Wildflowers grow free from the earth, like your hair is growing back after chemo. This year, both of us have gone suddenly grey. Or is it silver, daisy-white? In that field in our future, we'll compare what's grown from the earth and what's grown from us.

We will not have each other forever. That's what this year told us. Not like a theory, and not like a metaphor. Like, we found out there were so many ways to lose, and one way is that the losses don't end. The night your mother died, my aunt died. And it went on like that, my small tragedies synced to your devastating news, leaving us in our sickbeds at the same time. And then we'd be eating the same vegan ice cream when we'd call to talk about God: the god that lived in the last crescent of the moon, in the wild-flowers in your yard. You'd say: *we are in this together*, and maybe you meant all of us, everyone standing by the shore of Lake

Ontario, where you'd walk a few days after chemo, bathing in wind. *We are in this together:* us and that lake that sometimes tests toxic, then miraculously clean. When we were kids, the shoreline was always poisoned and the zebra mussels were everywhere; they cut your feet if you tried to wade in. But the city closed down enough factories, and it's changed like we have, it seems to be getting through.

We are in this together. Not because we face the same thing; we are in this together because we choose to be.

According to the Greeks, there are as many kinds of love as there are types of wildflower seeds, in the $1.99 packages you mailed me. There's *storge*, familial love; the love that we have across decades, generations. I see it in the coneflower that can make it through drought. And *eros*, the erotic: what else explains the lemon mint? The seed splits, the stalk grows, and all life is drawn to it. Bees cling to its blossoms forever. Borage; they've used that as a remedy for the heart for millennia. Warriors once ate the flowers before they went into battle: blue petals in their teeth as they held their swords. Those flowers grow where both our ancestors are from, in the Mediterranean. And even their name sounds like courage. Bees gather on these flowers, too, humming gently. The Greeks might say different, but I think these are the weeds of *philia*—brotherly love. That's what borage does: it befriends us; it gives itself to our literal hearts, then falls to seed and grows again, and again.

Borage, *philia*; cornflower, *storge*. You and I, we've lived plenty of what the Greeks describe. Which is how I know there is no partition, really: monocropping makes everything die, and the key to wildflowers is that they are wild. Platonic love is just a theory of Plato, who believed the mind was not the body, and the body was not a wildflower field.

Here's what I believe in: *agape*—that universal, unconditional love—love that transcends and persists. Some use this word to describe God, but I would use it for the meadow. Black-eyed Susan, butterfly weed: how we are loved by thee. Wild bergamot, catchfly, the bees crowding their legs with pollen. What else could it mean?

This is the magic: You plant the seeds, and it's not a symbol. You plant the actual seeds, and you find out what grows.

We are in this together because we choose to be. I don't think it has a singular name: the love that you choose to build your life on. Lemon mint grows in it, the bees come through, there are weeds everywhere and that's how you know it will survive.

We will not have each other forever. But we do have the car and directions to a nice river. And when we get there, the wildflowers will have risen, like our lives from the husk of this year, like your hair from the scalp of chemo, like the last of the virus from my lungs. As for the pain and suffering we've come through—you're right, it's enough. "Pass me the chips," I'll say in the field of our future, once the sun has dried us good enough and we are back in our dresses, with wildflowers lost through our hair, pressed to the warm skin of our backs. There is no perfect. No forever. We'll stay there until dusk sends us running to the car for blankets, then drive off into the sunset. Drive right into the sunset—*philia, eros, agape*—petals through our dresses, seeds stuck to the back of our knees, waiting for the moment they finally are shaken free.

THE
UNDERSTORY

Companion Essays and Additional Research

DEFORESTATION

On Zoonotic Disease and Global Health

I
F WE ARE living in an age of zoonosis, then we are also living in a time of uncertainty; personal uncertainty about our safety and health, and shared uncertainty about the impact of illness on our world's future. It makes sense to ask questions—deep questions—about how we got to this place, even if there aren't precise answers. What there are, it seems, are patterns. Patterns that will continue to grow unless fundamental changes are made.

In February 2021, the World Health Organization released initial conclusions on the origins of SARS-COV-2. Their global study was conducted with the aim to increase understanding of how the virus originated, improve global response to the current pandemic, and enhance the world's preparedness to future zoonotic spillover events. Ultimately, the results were cited as inconclusive, as an exact reservoir or spillover event could not be identified. This is not unique to COVID-19, and has been common with other coronaviruses, as well. The study did establish "exceedingly high" likelihoods for a zoonotic origin of COVID-19, with the highest likelihood being transmission through an "intermediate host." Relevant to the queries of "Deforestation," the WHO report spoke directly to the correlation between "spillover events" and "large-scale environmental and socioeconomic changes, including land use change, deforestation, agricultural expansion and intensification, trade in wildlife, and expansion of human settlements."[1]

The report concluded that "a laboratory origin of the pandemic was considered to be extremely unlikely."[2] It also stated: "Many of the early cases were associated with the Huanan market, but a similar number of cases were associated with other markets and some were not associated with any markets."[3]

These facts seem particularly important to point out in a global context where enormous attention has been focused on wildlife markets and the actions of individuals in China. Where the causes of zoonotic spillover events are known to be systemic, and rooted in top-down resource extraction, this discourse of individual responsibility is not only scientifically inaccurate, it is often implicitly—or explicitly—racist. It also does nothing to protect our world. Instead, like the denial of climate change, this discourse may maintain and reinforce the conditions that put us all at risk.

PRIOR TO THE pandemic, numerous efforts were already underway to establish shared policy frameworks, aimed at preventing and/or limiting the emergence of zoonotic diseases. In particular, the WHO and global NGOs have been calling for alignment with the "One Health" approach. Leading up to the convening of the World Health Assembly for a special session in 2021, a number of policy briefs were put forth discussing this multisectoral, transdisciplinary approach. These also affirmed the intimacy of pandemics and climate change. From the Global Health Centre's policy brief:

> The OH (One Health) approach recognizes that the health of all living organisms is interdependent, the product of connections among humans, animals, plants, and the environment they share. The COVID-19 pandemic and other emerging infectious diseases (EIDS), as well as well-established endemic zoonoses and the continuing threat of antimicrobial resistance, demonstrate the importance of the connections between the health of animals and humans, as they interact with and within their shared environment, and of the urgent need to address human, animal, and environmental health challenges holistically. Among EIDS, up to 75 percent result from infectious agents of animal origin that may be able to infect and spread among humans .... Deforestation and other land use changes also play important roles in the emergence of new infectious agents, including by fuelling climate change, which is closely linked to the emergence, re-emergence, and establishment of infectious diseases (e.g., post-flooding cholera outbreaks and changes in parasite and vectors host ranges), as well as an alarming loss of biodiversity.[4]

The special session of the World Health Assembly, which took place from November 20 to December 1, 2021, was held to discuss the creation of a legally binding global Pandemic Treaty. The result of the special session was an agreement to establish a "new instrument" to enact shared policy—versus *binding* policy—the basis of which is yet to be determined.[5] In addition to crucial health measures, this kind of agreement could establish new global environmental policies aimed at preventing future zoonotic spillover events. But it is important to note that distinct concerns are being raised about how a mechanism like this could—and likely would—reinforce global inequalities that have been brought to light, and made worse, by the pandemic itself. As clearly put by Obijiofor Aginam, an expert in global health governance from the United Nations University:

> Nothing about COVID-19 changes how global health governance reflects "embedded interests and structures … that privilege the most powerful states and non-state actors." With the pandemic battering high-income countries and multinational corporations, these actors have heightened incentives to leverage their advantages in the INB (Intergovermental Negotiating Body) to get what they want and limit constraints on their behaviour.[6]

On RCMP Violence: A Note

ROYAL CANADIAN Mounted Police (RCMP) violence against Indigenous land defenders on Turtle Island is widespread and ongoing. Speaking to this in a published book is difficult because these notes could—and should—be updated every few months to reflect new contexts, and require much more extensive discussion of relationship, beyond the scope of this essay collection. For ongoing coverage, I commonly look to independent media sources like *The Tyee* and *The Narwhal*, which often have reporters on the ground, and also redirect to the websites and press releases of Nations and communities involved.

In summer 2021, RCMP violence was most prevalent at the Ada'itsx/Fairy Creek watershed. As I write this note in December

2021, the most extensive and recent acts of RCMP violence have taken place in relationship to the Coastal GasLink pipeline, where arrests of Indigenous elders and land defenders, legal observers and members of the media have been ongoing in Wet'suwet'en territory. These actions stand in direct contravention to rulings by the Supreme Court of Canada, as well as the United Nations Declaration on the Rights of Indigenous Peoples, which the government of British Columbia itself passed into law in 2019. Specifically, in 1991, a landmark Supreme Court of Canada ruling confirmed Wet'suwet'en and Gitxsan Rights and Title. In 2020, Wet'suwet'en Hereditary Chiefs issued an eviction notice to the Coastal GasLink pipeline company, citing this ruling. This eviction notice was enforced with blockades, beginning in November 2021, and ricochet of RCMP violence and illegal arrests followed. From the press release connected to original eviction notice:

> Canada's courts have acknowledged in Delgamuukw-Gisdaywa v. The Queen that the Wet'suwet'en people, represented by our hereditary chiefs, have never ceded nor surrendered title to the 22,000 square kilometres of Wet'suwet'en territory. The granting of the interlocutory injunction by BC's Supreme Court has proven to us that Canadian courts will ignore their own rulings and deny our jurisdiction when convenient, and will not protect our territories or our rights as Indigenous peoples.
>
> Anuc 'nu'at'en (Wet'suwet'en law) is not a "belief" or a "point of view." It is a way of sustainably managing our territories and relations with one another and the world around us, and it has worked for millennia to keep our territories intact. Our law is central to our identity. The ongoing criminalization

of our laws by Canada's courts and industrial police is an attempt at genocide, an attempt to extinguish Wet'suwet'en identity itself.[1]

REWILDING

On Silence

READING ANNIE DILLARD—*Nature's silence is its one remark*—I wondered how silence might act as a keystone. In silence, could we find our place with what is silent, with the unlanguageable world? (Here, I'm referencing something different than audible noise and verbal speech. I'm referencing the shared meanings and set definitions that create language itself. I'm saying: what if that all dropped away?[1]) No doubt, this would create a trophic cascade: instant change, disassembled systems, a burgeoning of chaos where there is currently control. If the goal of a human *rewilding* is to "unhuman" ourselves—to turn from the brick and misaligned mortar of civilization—the loss of a shared language might do it. We might quickly ebb ourselves into the unringing bell of nature's silence; like moss covering a fallen tree branch, like fungi eating a decaying body, our voices turned to soil, to the understory of the forest.

But is that the goal? To *unhuman*, to rise above, to burgeon into chaos? To re-create—to enact upon our bodies and lives—the impact of a storm?

I have learned there is a whiplash to chaos. When hurricanes hit where I was staying, when lava covered my aunt's home, when a winter storm took out power and water to my house for ten days: the army was the first force called in. In dark green, in badges, they waded through floods, belted with guns. I remember them standing by the edge of a newly formed lagoon, only the treetops rising from the water, and mist all around us, on the Big Island of Hawaii. Or police standing by huge fallen trees on the road, waiting for hired men with chainsaws, as the snow fell on my stalled car, on Salt Spring Island. Those men were the best prepared for the job—that's the truth—those forces are designed for emergency measures. And I almost didn't care who they were, if they could get us heat and running water; if they could airlift my aunt and her neighbours from their homes, when the lava suddenly closed in. But of course it matters, and it's more than a symbol. This is a key way settler nation states maintain power. Imminent change meets eminent domain: stolen land reclaims itself, and then the state reclaims it, over and over. With law and with language, with story and with force.

NATURAL DISASTERS DO not act as keystones: they reinforce extractive systems, they reinforce the state. The loss of human life is not a metaphor or a symbol for personal transformation. Wreckage is not the same as rewilding. It is important to say this directly because the opposite is also being said—in *#rewilding*, in "new age" movements, and in narratives about overpopulation. To claim overpopulation is the problem is to claim we all walk this earth the same way, and we do not. The systems that cause the most harm to the planet are the least impacted by these events, and the individuals who cause the least damage carry the greatest burden and experience the greatest loss of life and livelihood—despite what Jane Goodall once said at the World Economic Forum: "All these [environmental] things we talk about wouldn't be a problem if there was the size of population that there was 500 years ago."[2]

What was she proposing, exactly? What did she intend to imply, when she said this to a global forum of economic leaders?

This is the place where rewilding can leave functional ecology and meet eco-fascism. One discourse enters the other, insidiously and quickly: if overpopulation is the problem, if humans act as deer do in an ecosystem, and predators can create a trophic cascade that enacts alignment, a false equivalency can follow. Say: a hurricane is like a predator, an earthquake is like a wolf, and herds of us need to go so the forest can regrow, so the banks can restabilize, so the earth itself can survive; and then it isn't so bad—it's natural, even, when a natural disaster happens—that's rewilding. But that is not rewilding—a restoration that implies, specifically, systems change—that's eugenics. Eugenics: the ideology and practice, rising from fascism and Nazism, that the systematic loss of selections of the population will improve conditions for future generations. The costs and impacts of climate change sit along distinct borders of race, class, disability, and citizenship. There is no neutrality or generalization possible when speaking about overpopulation.

THE WOLVES IN Yellowstone were not a metaphor, or a symbol; they were literal wolves. The deer and carrion were deer and carrion. What I'm seeking in myself is not a way to dissolve the human from within, a way to turn from the door of my species and the systems we've built. I'm looking, instead, for a way to belong in a world that I can't quite comprehend; seeking a home that is not on stolen land, but in my own queer, disabled body and neurodivergent mind.

So, here's what I come to: our silence might lead us into relationship with the unspeaking world, but not one another. This is what Dillard means, I think. The fact that we differ from nature's silence—that we can be in relationship with it, and not *it*—that's the beauty. Not a turning away from the human within us, not an absence, not a burgeoning of chaos: but a shift in how we make meaning. To make meaning from this silence is also to make meaning of our voice. If we do not respond when the fixed point of language breaks, then who does? Maybe only the army, to clear the road and bring water. Maybe only the nation state.

In a speech to the National Book Foundation, Ursula K. Le Guin once said: "We live in capitalism, its power seems inescapable—but then, so did the divine right of kings. Any human power can be resisted and changed by human beings. Resistance and change often begin in art. Very often in our art, the art of words."[3]

ALL BRIDGES ARE both receptive and active. If listening is my keystone, it has an active counterpart, I think, in speech. Silence and listening; sound and speaking: these elements fitting together not as a dichotomy but as interplay, as ecosystem, as carbon to oxygen, as music. Music, Mozart famously said, is found in the space between notes. And it's like that, I think: the space where you and I meet, and don't meet, and our unknowable future, and our untouchable now. Perhaps all we really share is that low thrum of silence, nature's unspeaking voice, which whispers that we are never alone. Maybe we can meet in that gap, in the gully, beyond the cliff's edge where I once turned from my fear.

Begin by listening, I tell myself. *Begin your stories here.* And into that space: an entire world appears.

LAZARUS SPECIES

On the Endangered Species Act:
Black-Footed Ferret v. Pipeline

A s I conducted my research into the Lazarus rise of the black-footed ferret, I threaded through old records—research papers, interviews, and VHS-derived videos of the conservationists in action, holding antennas in the prairie fields at night to track the radio collars of the ferrets in motion. One question continued to pull at my attention: Were the ferrets really extinct to *everyone* in 1979?

In 1985, a journalist from the *Los Angeles Times* interviewed John Hogg, the rancher who found the first Lazarus ferret, and nearby rancher Jack Turnell. Turnell suggested that "other ranchers may have observed signs of the ferrets on their ranches but kept it quiet." Turnell is also quoted as saying: "a lot of ranchers would feel uneasy about federal and state people coming and going all the time.... Some might even fear having their ranch shut down to protect an endangered species."[1]

When Congress passed the Endangered Species Act (ESA) in 1973, it established new laws and restrictions on private land use, increasing the state's ability to intervene and even enact the law of Eminent Domain, reclaiming private property.[2] One can see why ranchers might have been hesitant about reporting endangered species, given this fact—but it may have been worse than that.

In 1986, the *New York Times* suggested: "At best, ranchers who want unimpeded use of their land have been known to keep the presence of an endangered species as quiet as possible. At worst, they have resorted to 'shoot and shovel,' discreetly and illegally disposing of a bald eagle or a grizzly bear, lest some official or animal conservation activist start calling for creation of a refuge there."[3]

In particular, protection of the black-footed ferret in the Midwest could—and actively did—prevent the most lucrative use of land in Wyoming: drilling for oil and laying pipeline. The ESA established—and has maintained—federal restrictions on where and how land can be developed for large-scale resource extraction. In an old video produced by Wyoming's Fish and Wildlife Service, a conservationist stands in a field with a mountain behind him, recalling the rediscovery of the ferret. Though the ferrets had been declared extinct two years before, the land still needed to be surveyed for the species before development.

"This would have been in 1981," he says in the film, "and we were conducting pipeline surveys. There was a big gas pipeline that was between Rock Springs and Rawlins, and we, the Fish and Wildlife Service, had been contracted to go and look for ferrets along this pipeline corridor. So we were just about finishing that project up when we made our typical report in to our supervisor, and then he informed us at that time that there had been a ferret discovered in the Meeteetse area."[4]

The ferrets were not discovered directly along the planned pipeline corridor—they were found three hundred miles away—but I still find the connection striking because of the timing. The man is asking the land if pipeline can run through it—he's literally in the field—when the black-footed ferret rises again. If ferrets had been found in the surveyed area, it would have been a faceoff between Fish and Wildlife and the lobbying power of oil and gas in Wyoming. It would have been *Black-Footed Ferret v. Pipeline*.

This is all conjecture; I'm sitting here with my questions, because questions are what I have. But these questions are still relevant today, in the context of *keystone* species, and the *Keystone* XL pipeline. From the Keystone XL Right-of-Way Application, January 17, 2020:

> Six species that are federally listed as threatened and endangered under the ESA (whooping crane, black-footed ferret, interior least tern, piping plover, northern long-eared bat, and rufa red knot) and 36 listed as BLM special status species have been identified to potentially occur on federal lands crossed by the Project.[5]

These types of environmental evaluations are required due to current ESA regulations. This one, prepared by EXP Energy Services, concludes there is likely no impact on the ferrets—which is unsurprising, given how endangered they are, and how few currently exist in the wild. These reports are not required to speak to the future, however; how the pipeline might impede—or make impossible—the return of the ferrets to the wild. Ultimately, for Keystone XL to move forward, its best that both keystone and endangered species are long gone from the area—and best that they do not return.

But highly endangered species—even those declared extinct—do return sometimes; rising from the depths of the ocean, a tiny stream, or a humble prairie dog burrow. And this fact could shape our future world in profound, unexpected ways. Federal laws connected to the Endangered Species Act are increasingly at risk of being overturned, but as of the writing of this book, most of them hold. In the past, these regulations have posed some of the strongest legal challenges to pipeline proposals, and have been able to stall or halt their production.

This is particularly relevant in contexts where Indigenous land rights and sovereignty continue to be violated, and where legal frameworks in the United States are lacking. Recent lawsuits have been filed based on ESA laws to halt pipeline production, specifically to reinforce the work of land defenders, in ongoing movements such as Standing Rock.[6] Undoubtedly, more lawsuits of this kind will follow. Should a black-footed ferret be found rising from a Lazarus nest in the vicinty, it will be *Black-Footed Ferret v. Keystone XL*—and for now, there is legal precedent for the ferret to win.

On the Business of De-Extinction

A S PREVIOUSLY STATED, the birth of Elizabeth Ann was accomplished through a multiyear partnership between Revive & Restore, United States Fish and Wildlife Service, San Diego Zoo Global, the Association of Zoos and Aquariums, and the for-profit company ViaGen Pets & Equine, with the aim of increasing the future genetic diversity of the black-footed ferret, and as a result, increasing the likelihood of the species' survival. And to restate: the work of ViaGen Pets & Equine, in particular, carries a high level of controversy. I wanted to look further into these partnerships, to understand the interests that might be at play: where the money lines lead to the bloodlines of Elizabeth, Streisand's dogs, and maybe, the woolly mammoths of our future.

As a result of being a for-profit company, ViaGen has undergone a number of changes over the past decade with regards to ownership, first amalgamating with Start Licensing, who already held three key cloning patents. According to 2020 financial statements, ViaGen then became a fully owned subsidiary of Precigen Inc., a biopharmaceutical company focused on the research and development of human cell and gene therapy. One of the first operating principals mentioned on Precigen's website is: "fiscal strength: responsible capital allocation to ensure runway for maximum value creation."[1]

On the other end of this relationship puzzle, are those who are currently using Viagen's technology. Sooam Biotech Research Foundation in South Korea licenses their technology from Start Licensing, the above-mentioned subsidiary of ViaGen, who owns the cloning patent.[2] The surgeon leading for-profit dog cloning services at Sooam is Hwang Woo-suk. Woo-suk is a well-known scientist due to the fact that in 2004, he put forth claims in the international journal *Science* that he had successfully cloned the first-ever human embryo. Specifically, Woo-suk claimed to have created embryonic stem cells by somatic cell nuclear transfer, the same process that was used to create Dolly the Sheep and Elizabeth Ann. However, in 2006, it was shown that this was "fabricated," and that Woo-suk had engaged in "research misconduct." As a result, in 2009, Woo-suk was convicted of embezzlement and bioethics violations and sentenced to two years in prison.[3]

Sooam Biotech is just one example of where and how ViaGen's technology is being used. It is a fraught example, one that plays deeply to my concerns about the intersection of medical ethics and commercial interests.

The work of Revive & Restore seems to differ greatly from the aforementioned companies. Particularly, it is a nonprofit organization that appears to be built on relationships across sectors, with both state, nonprofit and for-profit actors, rather than existing as an independent, highly funded research facility. As such, understanding Revive & Restore's work, and how they might accomplish revival and restoration, seems to require looking at these relationships. Not so much Ben Novak and his future dating profile (which might read: *love woolly mammoths?* SWIPE RIGHT); more the board of directors.

As mentioned before, the cofounder, executive director, and president of the board of Revive & Restore is Ryan Phelan, who is described as a "serial entrepreneur, active in the for-profit and nonprofit world." Her company DNA Direct, which was like a smaller, medically focused version of Ancestry.com and 23andMe, sold to pharmacy benefit manager Medco Health Solutions, Inc. in a closed deal in 2010.[4] This gives me pause—a long pause— because, again, a widely raised concern is that personalized genetic testing and profiling could lead to discrimination by health care companies; specifically that they could limit the drugs and procedures they cover based on DNA records.

The terms of the sale of DNA Direct are closed; all I have is speculation. Speculation, questions. What kind of data did Medco get? What are they going to do with it? The answer could be something magnanimous, for all I know. But again, I don't know. If I'd sent them my DNA, I wouldn't quite know, either, because that is part of the bargain for $69. What I *do* know is this: genebanks make *bank*. In the midst of the pandemic, Ancestry.com sold to Blackstone Investment Group for $4.7 billion. 23andMe then went public with the help of Virgin Media's Richard Branson, valued at $3.5 billion. This followed 23andMe's previous investment by Google.

I can see why Medco would want access to DNA Direct's records; it's less clear why media moguls like Richard Branson are investing in banks of human genome data like they're the next Snapchat. On the whole, it seems like they're hedging bets—and to me, that's crossing a line. A line that entangles our DNA with a stock price, and leaves those stocks encoded with the very numbers that make us up. RNA, DNA—DOW.

The truth is that I don't even know *what I don't know* of this picture. No one really does; that's the caution being given in the field of bioethics. And while that does not mean what is happening is horribly wrong, it does mean that we, as a global population, have little agency and barely any decision-making power when it comes to the buying and trading of human DNA. And there are no signs that animal DNA—rare, endangered, or extinct animal DNA—will be regulated better. How are extinct passenger pigeons going to advocate for themselves?

"It all sounds like *Jurassic Park*," the FAQ on Revive & Restore's website reads, "How is this different?" The answer, I think, is that it *isn't* that different. Revival is an idea, a story, like any scientific theory before it's made manifest. What's different between *Jurassic Park* and Revive & Restore is that *we* are not a movie. Our DNA is more than a code or a stock. So, I don't think biotech progress is bad, or wrong, or should be outright avoided. But I do think it should be questioned, and held to more account than a fictional theme park.

There are parts of this world that are unquantifiable, invisible; things that cannot be put on a spreadsheet or even given language. And I think those things should be protected. Like the natural lifespan of our pets, however much we love them. Like the threshold of death; I do think that is sacred. Even if it carries the weight of extinction. Because what we call *Lazarus species* have only risen from a story we told about them. The black-footed ferret was always alive.

MOUNTAIN THAT
EATS MEN

On the Lithium Coup

A S PREVIOUSLY STATED, Bolivia has endured nearly two hundred coup d'états since the official declaration of independence in 1825. The Spanish Empire enforced and maintained systems of centralized power in order to extract silver from Cerro Rico over hundreds of years. And that centralized power, centralized wealth, centralized military strength—alongside strong foreign interest in Bolivian resources—did not disappear in 1825. Instead, Bolivia became a nation with a singular name and deeply divided communities. On the one hand, the wealthier descendants of the Spanish, who continue to be largely located in the

Santa Cruz region, and often show political support for the privatization of national resources; and on the other, the Indigenous
majority of Bolivia, who live throughout the Altiplano and
mountain regions, and continue to fight for their way of life as
Indigenous peoples, and their rights as miners, cocaleros, and
farmers.[1] Often, the coups in Bolivia are attributed to conflict
between these groups surrounding the use and extraction of
resources—with tension amplified by foreign intervention.
Specifically, there is clear documentation of the United States'
financial involvement in the 1971 military coup in Bolivia that first
brought Hugo Banzer to power.[2]

For almost two hundred years, these coups resulted in a con-
tinual exchange of power between the wealthy elite of Santa Cruz
and central military forces. The election of Evo Morales and his
party in 2005, on a platform of reclaiming control of national
resources, and as a member of the Indigenous majority, was a significant shift from this history. But after three presidential terms,
President Morales resigned in November 2019, in the wake of
twenty-one days of widespread protests questioning the legitimacy of the national election, and the military calling for him to
step down.

The international community remains divided about whether
these events constitute a coup or a crisis caused by justified
allegations of election fraud. When Morales fled to asylum in
Mexico, Jeanine Áñez Chávez, from the opposing political party,
declared herself interim president despite an absence of legisla-
tive quorum. But prior to November, the integrity of the election
was already in question. Morales was seen to have undermined
his own legitimacy, nationally and internationally, with his deci-
sion to amend the constitution and run for a fourth term, even

after a referendum determined he should not be allowed to do so.

The allegations of election fraud were initiated by the US-backed Organization of American States (OAS), headquartered in Washington, D.C.—at a time when Donald Trump and the GOP were in office—stating there had been a "clear manipulation" of the election results. The claim that there was overwhelming evidence of election fraud was reported internationally, and contributed to widespread protests in Bolivia. In contrast, however, researchers at MIT's Election Data and Science Lab, working with the independent Centre for Economic and Policy Research in Washington, concluded that the US-backed OAS study was flawed, stating that there was no statistical evidence of fraud.[3] This conclusion was echoed by numerous academics and institutions.

In response to these concerns, the OAS claimed MIT's study was itself flawed, though their response came without clear data. And at this point, the conversation enters a loop: Was the election fraudulent? Was the claim of fraud fraudulent? Was the claim that the fraud was fraudulent, fraudulent? It is like a mirror facing a mirror. There's no clear end. But the truth is, if you say *fraud, false, faulty* enough times, it will echo. The language overtakes the data—not completely, but enough to create doubt.

This strategy—of using *fraud* as a refrain, as a chorus—was seen en masse across the United States, used by Donald Trump and the GOP, beginning around the time of the Bolivian election in the fall of 2019 and continuing throughout 2020. So, the narrative about Bolivia belongs to a much bigger context, one that is waiting on the horizon, when Morales flees to Mexico and Chávez takes power.

Morales and his party, Movimento al Socialismo (MAS), have continued to assert that what took place in 2019 was a coup, and that it came as the result of foreign interest in Bolivia's natural resources—both those that have long been exploited, like silver and gas, and those foreign interests are just beginning to tap, like the lithium found in the flats south of Potosí. In the days that followed Morales's removal from office, many corporations with mining interests that aligned with the resources in Bolivia—such as Tesla, whose cars depend on lithium batteries, as well as the Silver Sands project—saw their stocks rise substantially, and then continue to rise.

In October 2020, new elections were held and Morales's party, MAS, returned to power with a majority, under the new leadership of Luis Arce. No irregularities were noted in this election, and it was lauded by the international community as democratic and fair. This gives more weight, however, to the notion there was no election fraud in 2019. Specifically, many of the voting "irregularities" that the Organization of American States (OAS) pointed out in 2019 review remained present in the so-called democratic and fair elections in 2020. This indicated that the voting patterns were not irregular, but ongoing. Of note, from the report published by the Centre for Economic and Policy Research:

> The communities targeted in the OAS analysis are … in the majority of cases, predominantly Indigenous. Though it may come as a shock to see a candidate receive 100 percent of the votes, it shouldn't. Community voting—in which a community comes to a consensus around who to vote for—is a widely recognized phenomenon in Bolivia.[4]

BLOOD STONES:
AN INVENTORY

On Diamonds

1. CONFLICT DIAMONDS

A S STRUGGLES FOR independence grew on the African continent in the 1950s, the market for diamonds also rose, thanks to De Beers' marketing campaigns, increasing their already substantial political influence and power. This had a far-reaching impact on democratic transitions across the continent. Many of De Beers' mining operations and extraction contracts were established in the early 1900s with the colonial powers, specifically for extractive financial gain. In the case of Angola, for example—one of the most significant sources of conflict diamonds—De Beers had established a contract with the Portuguese colonial government in 1917 that may have effectively allowed them to become a "de facto government with the ability to enforce laws and control security."[1]

When the colonial government was finally disestablished in Angola, diamond mining remained a singular source of established revenue for the liberated nation—and De Beers, a singular option for partnership, as they maintained a monopoly on the trade. De Beers remained actively involved with the political and economic landscape of Angola in the decades that followed— including a twenty-five year period of civil war. It is widely documented that the corporation, seeking to maintain their global monopoly and inflated prices, purchased the entire stock of diamonds that came from rebel-occupied mines in Angola. In doing so, they knowingly helped funnel an estimated $3.7 billion into the UNITA-led rebel movement, further destabilizing the democracy in Angola, and directly funding a war that resulted in over three hundred thousand deaths.[2]

This pattern of events was not exclusive to Angola. A similar history of entanglement can be seen in Sierra Leone, where civil war broke out in 1991. De Beers' purchasing of diamonds that directly fuelled and funded civil wars only ended when UN sanctions began in 1998, at which point De Beers' campaigned in *favour* of these sanctions, and condemned the very trade practices they'd built.[3]

2. BLOOD DIAMONDS

THE FILM *Blood Diamond* bought the topic of conflict diamonds to Hollywood in 2006. The civil war in Sierra Leone, and the way in which it was funded by diamond mining, was made famous by the movie, which starred Leonardo DiCaprio and earned him an Oscar nomination. In the film, a pink diamond is both the protagonist and antagonist; the conflict and the catalyst; and ultimately—in classic Hollywood form—the solution and salvation for DiCaprio. The singularity of De Beers is not clearly depicted in the movie, and the film doesn't cover their expansive legacy of extraction. But even with this misdirect and vagueness, the movie still had a purpose. In an industry fuelled by symbol, the film popularized an image you could not easily look away from: *blood* on a diamond, literal *blood*. Combined with De Beers' slogan, this idea was a disaster for the market: *the blood on your diamond is forever.*

Reportedly, De Beers and the World Diamond Council lobbied for a rewrite to the script before the movie came out. Specifically, they lobbied for additional mention of the Kimberley Process Certification Scheme (KPCS), an agreement established by the UN General Assembly in 2003 and aimed at preventing the sale of diamonds from countries with ongoing civil wars.

"We want people who see the movie to understand it is the past," said Cecilia Gardner, an attorney with the World Diamond Council, in an interview when the movie was debuting. "Lots has happened since that time."[4]

Gardner's claim is vague—and still, contraversial. By voluntarily signing onto the accord, nations can avoid embargos and continue their diamond trade with nations like the United States.

But KPCS only dictates embargos be placed in the context of civil war, like the ones that have taken place in Angola or Sierra Leone. Other contexts of state violence and human rights abuses do not contravene KPCS; these states remain eligible to export and trade *conflict-free* diamonds.[5]

For this reason, among others, many organizations see KPCS overall as a failure, specifically with regards to its impact on the stability of political infrastructure, safety, and quality of life for citizens. On the ground, for people in communities and nations where extraction continues, the realities may be the same as they were in the 1990s; realities of extreme human rights abuses, ongoing violence, and high environmental costs.

Global Witness, a UK-based NGO and mining watchdog, conducted the original research into conflict diamonds in Angola in 1998. They were instrumental is establishing the need for a global framework and influencing decision-making in the United Nations. But in 2011, Global Witness removed themselves from the Kimberley Process, stating:

> Nearly nine years after the Kimberley Process was launched, the sad truth is that most consumers still cannot be sure where their diamonds come from, nor whether they are financing armed violence or abusive regimes.... The scheme has failed three tests: it failed to deal with the trade in conflict diamonds from Côte d'Ivoire, was unwilling to take serious action in the face of blatant breaches of the rules over a number of years by Venezuela and has proved unwilling to stop diamonds fueling corruption and violence in Zimbabwe. It has become an accomplice to diamond laundering—whereby dirty diamonds are mixed in with clean gems.[6]

The policy framework for KPCS has not radically shifted since then. The ethical sourcing of diamonds remains difficult to determine and is highly dependent on the consumer; a consumer who consistently faces what has been called the most effective advertising in the world. De Beers' new measure-in-progress is to use blockchain technology to directly mark the mine that a diamond is sourced from in its country of origin, so the customer can have more information at their fingertips. How this might resolve what the Kimberley Process cannot—for example, the ground transfer of diamonds across borders before they are locally stamped—remains to be seen, as does the answer to the more substantial question of the continued relationship between foreign resource extraction and the erosion of democratic institutions.

3. CANADIAN DIAMONDS

ETHICAL AND FAIR: these are subjective terms we live with—designed more for branding than policy; more for customers than miners. Even within the one global framework we have—the KPCS—what is being measured is not *ethics* but conflict. And by *conflict*, KPCS only means war. In this subjectivity and vagueness, many people suggest the best way to know if a stone is ethically sourced is to verify where it is from and check the state of democracy, human rights, and environmental protections there. Very often, it is suggested that diamonds and gemstones from Canada are among the most *ethical, conflict-free,* and *environmentally friendly* in the world. But like many people living within the borders of this country, I can quickly see what is missing from that designation.

De Beers operated an open pit diamond mine in Northern

Ontario, on Attawapiskat First Nation territory, from 2007 to 2019—less than one hundred kilometres from where the community lives; a community facing a systematic lack of access to clean drinking water. It is estimated the Nation received less than 0.5 percent royalties, approximately $2 million per year, while the mine generated approximately $400 million per year in diamond profit. It was also discovered that De Beers paid only $226 dollars in royalties to the province of Ontario from 2013 to 2014.[7]

Indigenous-led blockades against the mine were ongoing throughout its operation, and lawsuits against De Beers have continued.[8] In 2021, De Beers pled guilty to failing to report mercury levels that had become present in the water system. The fine they faced was only $100, and an additional $50,000 tax-deductible donation to charity.[9]

Issues pertaining to the disposal of waste materials from the closed mine carry on as I write this. To reduce costs, De Beers is seeking to open a third landfill site for their mine tailings, and plans to place it on vulnerable wetlands, a crucial part of water systems for the community—and also, it has been stated, a vital place of spiritual and cultural importance to the Attawapiskat Cree people.[10] In a press release written by the Attawapiskat First Nation in 2020, Attawapiskat Chief David Nakogee said the following:

> De Beers has profited a lot from the Victor Diamond Mine and will profit even more.... These expensive diamonds come from my Nation's homeland, in our backyard, and yet we continue to live in horrendous conditions where we can't even drink the water here from the taps. We keep watching the wealth of our Traditional Territory, from the waters and

lands to the wildlife, get industrialized. We keep watching others walk off with the profits of that industrialization, leaving us to bear the burden and the waste. When De Beers has the money to transport, recycle and re-use materials, and to properly monitor the effects of the mine on the lakes and rivers, they must be required to do so. We will not tolerate excuses when so much is at stake.[11]

THE ROMANCE
OF FLOODS

On Structural Violence

*To perceive tourism as a social relation calls for its recognition as
a power relation; social interaction in tourism is an expression of
power differentials and asymmetries based on gender, race, ethnicity,
class, nationality, and sexuality.*

—Tamar Diana Wilson and Annelou Ypeij,
"Tourism, Gender, and Ethnicity"

STRUCTURAL VIOLENCE. I return to this
term, again and again, when I think of
tourism and the development aid com-
plex. In some ways the term needs no definition; it says exactly

what it is. Violence is built into the structures of our world—in tangible material ways, and in less tangible, immaterial ways. Political theorist Peter Uvin uses the term to speak to the "consolidation of extreme inequality, social exclusion, and assaults on dignity." This definition, which aligns with the analysis put forth by Wilson and Ypeij, recognizes meaningful agency, respect and recognition by others as fundamental human needs, and the structures that limit these—that maintain "assaults on dignity"— as fundamental forms of violence.[1]

Much of Uvin's work focuses on the context in Rwanda leading up to the genocide there, concluding: "Development aid greatly contributes to social inequality, both directly, by its own spending patterns which very largely favour the wealthier strata of society, and indirectly, through its support of mechanisms of exclusion and clientelism."[2]

When agency and meaningful change are granted to one group, while systematically withheld from another, it is a form of serious violence against the social, emotional, and spiritual lives of individuals. Our basic human needs involve food, water, and shelter—but also dignity, respect, recognition, and agency. We deserve, each of us, a way out of the flood.

The helicopters flying above Cuiabá, as the waters rise: they can be understood as an attack against dignity, just as they are a symbol of social exclusion, and a sign of the wealth gap in Brazil, which is one of the highest in the world.[3] These helicopters are always flying in Brazil—over Rio, over São Paulo—filled with state police, or businessmen on their way to work, high above the favela hills. And rather than break down these structural divisions, which lay at the heart of the problem in Brazil, development aid often reinforces fragmentation and harm to material conditions (increased divisions in wealth and resources), and immaterial conditions (wellness of mind, spirit, and meaning).

As volunteers, as volun*tour*ists, our part in structural violence is often intimate and close—entangled with love, even. Or in Mary's case, a child. Twenty years and one pregnancy scare later, Derich and I are still friends. But even after two decades, I am still learning what I have to learn; still deciphering what happened between us that spring.

RARE HONEY

On Survival

WHEN GABOR MATÉ writes about addiction, he is often drawing from the years he spent working in the Downtown Eastside (DTES) of Vancouver. He also writes through the lens of his own childhood in Nazi-occupied Budapest, a context shaped by genocide. Likewise, Indigenous-led organizations in the DTES speak to the role of acute and structural violence in creating the circumstances in this neighbourhood, where a large Indigenous community lives. In one interview, Michael Lascelles—executive director of Aboriginal Front Door, which works to support food security in the neighbourhood—said: "The residential schools, and everything that occurred in our lives here in Canada, is a consequence of genocide. ... So here at Main and Hastings street you can see the consequence of genocide. These symptoms of substance abuse, low self-esteem and all these other things, are symptoms of genocide."[1]

In line with this, when Gabor Maté wrote, "Addiction is not a choice anyone makes ... it's not a moral failure," he also implied it's not a moral success, or a sign of better character, if we've never struggled with drug use.[2] Likely, it's a sign we are resourced.

Substance Use Disorder is fundamentally a medical issue that is constantly treated as a moral one. Personally, I don't believe it was strength, or will, or effort alone that got me sober—strength and effort are everywhere in the Downtown Eastside. I had a buffer to make those things count—a buffer called whiteness, mostly; a buffer of settlership, and that helped me access the medical resources I needed, eventually.

ON THE HORIZON of these interviews, which took place in 2013, there is a bigger crisis looming. In 2016, British Columbia will declare a public health emergency as the supply chain of opioids is increasingly contaminated with fentanyl, carfentanyl, and other substances, causing constant overdoses. By 2021, over twenty thousand people will have died in B.C. due to preventable opioid-related drug poisoning.[3] This will continue to push forward decriminalization, but still, Insite and the community here will have to campaign for safe housing, dignified medical treatment, and safe supply.

Through it all, community-led projects will act as crucial resources throughout the Downtown Eastside. Hives for Humanity will go on, mostly led by residents like Ian. They'll build habitats for wild pollinators, as well, and transform the planters and hanging baskets in the neighbourhoods to grow forage. "A pollinator corridor," Sara called it, when we met.

After thirteen years of tireless advocacy, construction is starting on a social housing project at 58 Hastings that will include important community space and a new health clinic. Though in the end, it will still only provide 120 homes at welfare rates, in a community where thousands are without shelter.

OUR FUNDAMENTAL NEEDS—for food and water, shelter, care, and connection—those needs are shared and constant, and we are all working to meet them in whatever way we can. Sometimes the work of survival involves drug use. Sometimes, the work of survival involves bees. And maybe, in the garden beside Insite, it involves both.

Not why the addiction—I hear Maté's words echo—*why the pain.* And also, the words of Vandana Shiva: *Seed is not just the source of life, it is the very foundation of our being.* You plant the seeds and it's not just a symbol. That's what I try to remember: You plant the seeds, and you tend what grows.

ACKNOWLEDGEMENTS

A S I WROTE this book, I moved back to the city where I grew up. I took up residence just a few blocks from the broken-down house where I was born, nearly forty years ago, into a circle of underground midwives. I am deeply grateful to have returned to this place known as Toronto/Tkaronto, the traditional territory and home of many Nations, including the Mississaugas of the Credit, the Anishnabeg, the Chippewa, the Haudenosaunee, and the Wendat people. I aim for my work and my words to be in service of the community, living lands, and diverse ecosystems of this place, and I hope that my gratitude and responsibilities are reflected in the work that I create.

Where two ecosystems meet, the result is not a divided line but an ecotone, an in-between space of the highest biodiversity—like an estuary, a mangrove, grasslands. Ecotones can form between us, as well—that's what I believe—where our ideas, experiences, and stories meet. And so the hope of this work is connection; imperfect, in progress, connection. I want to thank each person who has read this book, and brought their own knowledge and experience to these pages.

I am profoundly grateful for the support I have received on this journey. I want to thank my agent Stephanie Sinclair for insight, vision, and tireless support; for believing in my work and its place in the world. Thank you to my editor Linda Pruessen, for going above and beyond, journeying with these essays from seed into flower. And thank you to Book*hug Press for bringing this book to life. In the words of Ursula K. Le Guin: *we need writers who can remember freedom.* Jay and Hazel, I see you creating room for this kind of writing every day, and I am proud and grateful to have you as my publishers. Additional thanks go to: The Canada Council for the Arts, the Ontario Arts Council, and the Toronto Arts Council for supporting this project; *The New Quarterly* for publishing previous versions of "The Romance of Floods" and "A Brief History of Mermaids"; *Briarpatch Magazine* for publishing "Rare Honey," and the beekeepers at Hives for Humanity for taking part in the article; and The Banff Centre, Artscape Gibralter Point, JOYA: AiR, and Wendy Littlefield for hosting me as this book came to life.

Interconnection is the heartwood of this book. This collection was written during a particularly trying time in the world—a time of isolation, loss, illness, and uncertainty. But these past two years have also been a testament to resilience and community care. Thank you to my mother Christine, the true champion of this book; and to my sister Teoma—sidekick in these stories, and forever a brave, creative force in my life. Mom: thanks for bringing us to protests since third grade, and raising us with enough imagination to believe you might become a seal, once we finally saw the ocean. Thank you to Andreas Schroeder, Kyo Maclear, Elysia Glover, Anthony Meza-Wilson, Marla Brennan, and the many brilliant writers in my life for offering inspiration, insight, guidance and support on this book. To my mentors Seraphina Capranos and Robert Birch, and the entire BC Reclaiming witchcraft community: thank you for showing me, again and again, how to turn toward the fire. And to my dear friends and chosen family: I carry you with me, wherever I go. In the words of Richard Bach: *There is no such thing as far away.* Let's go plant those wildflower seeds.

END NOTES

INTRODUCTION

1. Simon Lewis and Mark Maslin, *The Human Planet: How We Created the Anthropocene* (New Haven; London: Yale University Press, 2018).

DEFORESTATION

1. World Health Organization, *WHO-convened global study of origins of SARS-COV-2: China Part*, (Geneva: World Health Organization, March 2021), who.int/publications/i/itemwho-convened-global-study-of-origins-of-sars-cov-2-china-part.
2. "One Health Basics: Zoonotic Disease," Center for Disease Control and Prevention, cdc.gov/onehealth/basics/zoonotic-diseases.html.
3. Katharine S. Walter, et al., "Genomic insights into the ancient spread of Lyme disease across North America," *Nature Ecology & Evolution* 1, (2017): 1569–1576, doi.org/10.1038/s41559-017-0282-8.
4. Katharine S. Walter, et al., "Genomic insights into the ancient spread of Lyme disease across North America," *Nature Ecology & Evolution* 1, (2017): 1569–1576, doi.org/10.1038/s41559-017-0282-8.

5. Tedros Adhanom Ghebreyesus, "WHO Director-General's opening remarks at 27th Tripartite Annual Executive Committee Meeting World Organisation for Animal Health (OIE)," World Health Organization, February 17, 2021, who.int/director-general/speeches/detail/who-director-general-s-opening-remarks-at-27th-tripartite-annual-executive-committee-meeting-world-organisation-for-animal-health-oie-17-february-2021.

6. Tom Evans, Sarah Olson, James Watson, Kim Gruetzmacher, Mathieu Pruvot, Stacy Jupiter, Stephanie Wang, Tom Clements, and Katie Jung, "Links between ecological integrity, emerging infectious diseases originating from wildlife, and other aspects of human health—an overview of the literature," Wildlife Conservation Society, April 2020, doi.org/10.13140/RG.2.2.34736.51205.

LAZARUS SPECIES

1. On Keystone Species:

> Keystones species are often placed into five categories: 1) keystone predators, like the sea stars, wolves, and sea otters, who control over-population and maintain species diversity; 2) keystone prey, such as the Arctic krill for whales, or snowshoe hare for endangered lynx populations, that serve as critical—and often the only—food source to keystone predators; 3) mutualists, such as bees and hummingbirds, whose interaction with others is mutually beneficial and shapes entire ecosystems; 4) plants, such as maple, birch, and cherry trees, that provide both critical food and shelter for other keystone species; and 5) ecosystem engineers, such as bison and prairie dogs, who reshape the physical landscape around them.

Based on Melissa Denchak, "Keystone Species 101," National Resource Defence Council, September 9, 2019, nrdc.org/stories/keystone-species-101.

2. Dino Grandoni, "Ivory-billed woodpecker officially declared extinct, along with 22 other species," *Washington Post*, September 29, 2021, washingtonpost.com/climate-environment/2021/09/29/endangered-species-ivory-billed-woodpecker.

3. "FAQs Answered by Stewart Brand," Revive & Restore, reviverestore.org/faq.

4. "FAQs Answered by Stewart Brand," Revive & Restore, reviverestore.org/faq.

5. Norman F. Carlin, Ilan Wurman, and Tamara Zakim, "How to Permit Your Mammoth: Some Legal Implications of 'De-Extinction,'" *Stanford Environmental Law Journal* 33, no. 1 (2014), law.stanford.edu/publications/how-to-permit-your-mammoth-some-legal-implications-of-de-extinction/.

6. "Initiate Cloning," ViaGen Pets & Equine, viagenpets.com/product/initiate-cloning.

7. Bill Berkrot, "Medco Buys Genetic Services Company DNA Direct," Reuters, February 2, 2010, reuters.com/article/us-medco-dna-idUSTRE6110VE20100202.

8. "FAQs Answered by Stewart Brand," Revive & Restore, reviverestore.org/faq.

9. "Bringing Biotechnologies to Conservation," Revive & Restore, reviverestore.org.

10. Sabrina Imbler, "Meet Elizabeth Ann, the First Cloned Black-Footed Ferret," *New York Times*, February 18, 2021, nytimes.com/2021/02/18/science/black-footed-ferret-clone.html.

THE PLASTER CITIZENS OF POMPEII

1. P.J. Baxter, Willy Aspinall, A. Neri, Guilio Zuccaro, Robin Spence, Raffaello Cioni, and Gordon Woo, "Emergency Planning and Mitigation at Vesuvius: A New Evidence-Based Approach," *Journal of Volcanology and Geothermal Research* 178, no. 3 (2008): 454–73, doi.org/10.1016/j.jvolgeores.2008.08.015.

MOUNTAIN THAT EATS MEN

1. Jack Weatherford, *The History of Money* (New York: Random House, 1998); Patrick Greenfield, "Stories of Cities #6: How Silver Turned Potosí in the First City of Capitalism," *The Guardian*, March 21, 2016, theguardian.com/cities/2016/mar/21/story-of-cities-6-potosi-bolivia-peru-inca-first-city-capitalism.

2. For more on this, see: "From Rightist Chaos to Leftist Constitutionalism: The Institutionalization of Bolivian Populism," Council on Hemispheric Affairs, January 23, 2009, coha.org/from-rightist-chaos-to-leftist-constitutionalism-the-institutionalization-of-bolivian-populism; "A Brief Recent History of Bolivia and the Rise of President Morales," Council on Hemispheric Affairs, January 24 2009, coha.org/a-brief-recent-history-of-bolivia-and-the-rise-of-president-morales/; Brooke Larson, Raúl Madrid, René Antonio Mayorga, and Jessica Varat, "Bolivia: Social Movements, Populism, and Democracy," Woodrow Wilson Center, August 2008, wilsoncenter.org/publication/bolivia-social-movements-populism-and-democracy; Andrea Marston and Amy Kennemore, "Extraction, Revolution, Plurinationalism: Rethinking Extractivism from Bolivia," *Latin American Perspectives* 46, no. 2, (2019): 141–160, doi.org/10.1177/0094582X18781347.

3. Jim Shultz and Melissa Crane Draper, eds. "The Cochabamba Water Revolt and Its Aftermath" in *Dignity and Defiance: Stories from Bolivia's Challenge to Globalization* (Berkeley: University of California Press, 2008); William Finnegan, "Leasing the Rain," *The New Yorker*, April 8, 2002, newyorker.com/magazine/2002/04/08/leasing-the-rain; Raquel Gutiérrez Aguilar, *Rhythms of the Pachakuti: Indigenous Uprising and State Power in Bolivia* (Durham, NC: Duke University Press, 2014); Theodore H. MacDonald, "Inequity in Access to Water," in *Removing the Barriers to Global Health Equity* (Oxford: Radcliffe Publishing, 2008).

4. Sheraz Sadiq, "Timeline: Cochabamba Water Revolt," *PBS Frontline World*, June 2002, pbs.org/frontlineworld/stories/bolivia/timeline.html.

5. Juan Forero, "Bolivia's Cerro Rico: The Mountain That Eats Men," September 25, 2012, in *All Things Considered*, produced by NPR, radio, MP3 audio, 4:22, npr.org/2012/09/25/161752820/bolivias-cerro-rico-the-mountain-that-eats-men; Juan Forero, "Bolivia's Silver Mountain Loses Its Lustre as Report Warns of Risk of Collapse," *The Guardian*, October 2, 2012, theguardian.com/world/2012/oct/02/bolivia-potosi-mountain-silver-mining.

6. Kirsten Francescone, "Coeur Mines Treading in Dangerous Water at San Bartolome Mine in Bolivia," The Bullet, April 21, 2014, socialistproject.ca/2014/04/b971/; Kirsten Francescone, "Cooperative Miners and the Politics of Abandonment in Bolivia," *The Extractive Industry and Society* 2, no. 4: (2005): 746–55, doi.org/10.1016/j.exis.2015.10.004.

7. Wes Enzinna, "Thousands of Children as Young as 6 Work in Bolivia's Mines," interview by Arun Rath, November 30, 2013, in *All Things Considered*, produced by NPR, radio, MP3 audio, 4:58, npr.org/2013/11/30/247967228/thousands-of-children-as-young-as-6-work-in-bolivias-mines.

8. Mark Dickinson, "Touring Bolivia's Cerro Rico—The Mountain That Eats Men," *In the Fray*, December 31, 2019, inthefray.org/2019/12/touring-bolivia-cerro-rico-mountain-that-eats-men.

9. Samar Ahmad, "The Lithium Triangle: Where Chile, Argentina, and Bolivia Meet," *Harvard International Review*, January 15, 2020, hir.harvard.edu/lithium-triangle.

10. Jake Johnston and David Rosnick, "Observing the Observers: The OAS in the 2019 Bolivian Elections," Centre for Economic Policy Research, March 2020, cepr.net/wp-content/uploads/2020/03/bolivia-2020-3.pdf; Jake Johnston, "Data from Bolivia's Election Add More Evidence That OAS Fabricated Last Year's Fraud Claims," Centre for Economic Policy Research, October 21, 2020, cepr.net/data-from-bolivias-election-add-more-evidence-that-oas-fabricated-last-years-fraud-claims.

11. For more, see Evo Morales (@evoespueblo), ".@elonmusk, dueño de la fábrica más grande de autos eléctricos, dice sobre el golpe de Estado en #Bolivia: "Nosotros golpearemos a quien queramos". Otra prueba más de que el golpe fue por el litio boliviano; y dos masacres como saldo. ¡Defenderemos siempre nuestros recursos!" Twitter, July 25, 2020, twitter.com/evoespueblo/status/1287064230835957762.

12. "The 'Imperial City' is Reborn," *Financial Post*, August 13, 2020, financialpost.com/business-trends/the-imperial-city-is-reborn.

13. Simon Romero, "Eduardo Galeano, Uruguayan Voice of Anti-Capitalism, Is Dead at 74," *New York Times*, April 13, 2015, nytimes.com/2015/04/14/books/eduardo-galeano-uruguayan-voice-of-anti-capitalism-is-dead-at-74.html.

14. June Nash, *We Eat the Mines and the Mines Eat Us: Dependency and Exploitation in Bolivian Tin Mines* (New York: Columbia University Press, 1979), as quoted in Benjamin Dangl, "On Rituals and Revolutions in the Mines of Bolivia," ROAR *Magazine*, October 2, 2021, roarmag.org/essays/bolivia-miners-culture-resistance; see also: Raquel Gutiérrez Aguilar, *Rhythms of the Pachakuti: Indigenous Uprising and State Power in Bolivia* (Durham, NC: Duke University Press, 2014).

BLOOD STONES: AN INVENTORY

1. Hannah Elliot, "The Market for Crystals Is Outshining Diamonds in the Covid Era," *Bloomberg News*, May 28, 2020, bloomberg.com/news/articles/2020-05-28/no-longer-kooky-crystals-are-outshining-diamonds-in-the-covid-era; Stephen Robert Miller, "American Anxiety Drives a Crystal Boom: 'People Are Looking for Healing,'" *The Guardian*, October 31, 2020, theguardian.com/us-news/2020/oct/31/us-crystal-gem-boom-people-looking-for-healing; Eva Wiseman, "Are Crystals the New Blood Diamonds?" *The Guardian*, June 16, 2020, theguardian.com/global/2019/jun/16/are-crystals-the-new-blood-diamonds-the-truth-about-muky-business-of-healing-stones.

2. Tess McClure, "Dark Crystals: The Brutal Reality Behind a Booming Wellness Craze," *The Guardian*, September 17, 2019, theguardian.com/lifeandstyle/2019/sep/17/healing-crystals-wellness-mining-madagascar; Global Witness, "How Luxury Jewellers Risk Funding Military Abuses in Myanmar," December 15, 2021, globalwitness.org/en/campaigns/natural-resource-governance/conflict-rubies-how-luxury-jewellers-risk-funding-military-abuses-myanmar/.

3. "Syuw'em (History) of Xwaaqw'um Village," Xwaaqw'um, xwaaqwum.com/about/#history.

4. Alan Septoff, "A State of Ticking Time Bombs," Earthworks, June 25, 2020, earthworks.org/stories/minas-gerais-brazil/; Paul Robson, "The River Is Dead: The Impact of Catastrophic Failure of the Fundão Tailings Dam," London Mining Network, September 6, 2017, londonminingnetwork.org/wp-content/uploads/2017/09/Fundao-Report-Final-lowres.pdf.

5. Global Witness, "A Rough Trade: The Role of Companies and Government in the Angolan Conflict," December 1, 1998, cdn2.globalwitness.org/archive/files/pdfs/a_rough_trade.pdf; Lynne Duke, "Diamond Trade's Tragic Flaw," *Washington Post*, April 29, 2001, washingtonpost.com/archive/business/2001/04/29/diamond-trades-tragic-flaw/b4c2c3c4-f5a8-4ba7-9d96-c9a8f80945a1; Aryn Baker, "Blood Diamonds," *Time*, September 7, 2015, time.com/blood-diamonds.

6. Global Witness, "Jade: Myanmar's 'Big State' Secret," October 23, 2015, globalwitness.org/en/campaigns/oil-gas-and-mining/myanmarjade; Global Witness, "How Luxury Jewellers Risk Funding Military Abuses in Myanmar," December 15, 2021, globalwitness.org/en/campaigns/natural-resource-governance/conflict-rubies-how-luxury-jewellers-risk-funding-military-abuses-myanmar/; Global Witness, "War in the Treasury of the People: Afghanistan, Lapis Lazuli, and the Battle for Mineral Wealth," May 30, 2016, globalwitness.org/afghanistan-lapis.

THE ROMANCE OF FLOODS

1. On the Flooding in Cuiabá—News Reports from April 2001:

> "25 April 2001—Brazil—Flooding caused by heavy rains pounding western Brazil killed at least 13 people and left more than ten missing today, authorities said. The rains have not let up since the beginning of the week and have flooded several neighbourhoods in Cuiaba, about 700 miles north-west of Brasilia, and many residents had to be rescued by helicopter, civil defence said in a statement. The majority of the dead lived along the banks of rivers which overflowed, collapsing homes and dragging their victims downstream, the statement said. Despite the risk, thousands of people had climbed on top of their houses and were waiting for the police to rescue them ...."

> "26 April 2001—Torrential rain drowned at least 15 and turned 5,000 from their homes in Cuiaba, Brazil yesterday after more than a month's worth of rain fell in six hours over the city, local news reported. The Agencia Estado news service said two children were among the 15 who drowned and at least six people were still missing after waters rose well over 10ft in parts of the capital city of Mato Grosso state—about 940 miles from São Paulo."

From "Severe weather," *Disaster Prevention and Management* 10, no. 5 (December 2001), doi.org/10.1108/dpm.2001.07310eac.003.

A BRIEF HISTORY OF MERMAIDS

1. On the Origins of Atargatis:

> "At Ashkalon, where she was called Derketo, she seems to have appeared as half fish, a mermaid goddess. In De Dea Syria, Lucian reported that he saw a statue of a Phoenician goddess who was a mermaid; he confirmed that she was called Derketo. "

From Joanna Stuckey, "Atargatis, 'The Syrian Goddess,'" *Matrifocus* 8, no. 3 (2009), academia.edu/23577340/Atargatis_the_Syrian_Goddess_by_Johanna_Stuckey, drawing on: Douglas R. Frayne and Johanna H. Stuckey, *A Handbook of Gods and Goddesses of the Ancient Near East: Three Thousand Deities of Anatolia, Syria, Israel, Sumer, Babylonia, Assyria, and Elam* (Pennsylvania: Penn State University Press); Francis Redding Walton and Antony Spawforth, "Atargatis," *Oxford Classical Dictionary*, December 22, 2015, doi.org/10.1093/acrefore/9780199381135.013.896.

For more on this history, see: Harold W. Attridge and Robert A. Oden, eds., *The Syrian Goddess (De DeaSyria): Attributed to Lucian.* (Atlanta: Scholars Press/Society of Biblical Literature, 1976); Johanna Stuckey, "The Great Goddesses of the Levant," *Journal of the Society for the Study of Egyptian Antiquities* 29, (2002): 28-57.: 29, academia.edu/39990401/The_Great_Goddesses_of_the_Levant.

2. On the Queer History of *The Little Mermaid*:

> Hans Christian Andersen to the Grand Duke of Weimar, Oct 3, 1847, Copenhagen: "I love you as a man can only love the noblest and best. This time I felt that you were still more ardent, more affectionate to me. Every little trait is preserved in my heart. On that cool evening, when you took your cloak and threw it around me, it warmed not only my body, but made my heart glow still more ardently."

From Frederick Crawford, ed., *Hans Christian Andersen's Correspondence*, (London: Dean & Son, 1891); also cited in Rictor Norton, ed., *My Dead Boy: Gay Love Letter Through the Centuries* (San Francisco: Leyland Publications, 1998). See also: Brooke Allen, "The Uses of Enchantment," *New York Times*, May 20, 2001, archive.nytimes.com/www.nytimes.com/books/01/05/20/reviews/010520.20allent.html

RARE HONEY

1. For more on this, see: Nathan Crompton, Steffanie Ling, and Caitlin Shane, "Battle for 58 West Hastings: Broken Promises and Co-optation, 2016–2018," The Mainlander, June 19, 2018, themainlander.com/2018/06/19/58-west-hastings-2016-2018; Kai Rajala and Nathan Crompton, "Battle of 58 West Hastings: The History of a Fight for Housing, 2007–Present," The Mainlander, July 27, 2016, themainlander.com/2016/07/27/battleof58/; Harsha Walia, "Chronicles of the Olympic Tent Village," Vancouver Media Co-op, February 28, 2010, vancouver.mediacoop.ca/story/2908.

2. Gabor Maté (@gabormatemd), "Addiction is not a choice anyone makes …," Instagram photo, August 12, 2021, instagram.com/p/CSe7da_LYv1/.

3. For more on this, see: "The Incite Story," PHS Community Services Society, July 28, 2020, phs.ca/the-insite-story; "Vancouver's Approach to the Overdose Crisis," City of Vancouver, vancouver.ca/people-programs/drugs.aspx.

4. Dr. Vandana Shiva, as quoted in Taggart Siegel, ed., Queen of the Sun: What Are the Bees are Telling Us? (Sussex, UK: Clairview Books, 2012).

THE FAILSAFE

1. Charles Darwin, "Cell-Making Instinct of the Hive-Bee," in On The Origin of Species by Means of Natural Selection or The Preservation of Favoured Races in the Struggle for Life (London, UK: John Murray, 1859): 224.

2. Aristotle, Aristotle's History of Animals: In Ten Books, trans. Richard Cresswell (London, UK: George Bell & Sons, 1902); Shakespeare, Henry V, Act I, Scene 2, as quoted in Florian Maderspacher, "All the Queen's Men," Current Biology 17, no. 6 (March 20, 2007), doi.org/10.1016/j.cub.2007.02.017.

3. Charles Butler, The Feminine Monarchie, or a Treatise Concerning Bees (Oxford, UK: Joseph Barnes, 1609); Tammy Horn, Bees in America: How the Honey Bee Shaped a Nation (Lexington, KY: University Press of Kentucky, 2005).

4. J.H. Galloway, "The Industry of Bees," Gastronomica 7, no. 1 (2007): 100–103, doi.org/10.1525/gfc.2007.7.1.100; Everett Oertel, "History of Beekeeping in the United States," Agricultural Handbook, no. 335 (United States Department of Agriculture, 1980), ars.usda.gov/ARSUserFiles/60500500/PDFFiles/1-100/093-Oertel--History%20of%20Beekeeping%20in%20the%20U.S..pdf.

5. J.H. Cane and V.J. Tepedino, "Gauging the Effect of Honey Bee Pollen Collection on Native Bee Communities," Conservation Letters 10, no. 2 (2017): 205–210, doi.org/10.1111/conl.12263; Laura Russo, "Positive and Negative Impacts of Non-Native Bee Species around the World," Insects 7, no. 4 (November 28, 2016): 69, doi.org/10.3390/insects7040069.

6. "Bees Are Fundamental to Our Lives," Food and Agriculture Organization of the United Nations, May 21, 2021, fao.org/partnerships/container/news-article/en/c/1401610/; Emily Wilder, "Bees for Hire: California Almonds Becomes Migratory Colonies Biggest Task," & *The West*, Stanford University, August, 17, 2018, andthewest.stanford.edu/2018/bees-for-hire-california-almonds-become-migratory-colonies-biggest-task.

7. Matthew L. Forister, Emma M. Pelton, and Scott H. Black, "Declines in Insect Abundance and Diversity: We Know Enough to Act Now," *Conservation Science and Practice* 1, no. 8 (June 22, 2019), doi.org/10.1111/csp2.80.

8. Annette McGivney, "Like Sending Bees to War: The Truth Behind Your Almond Milk Obsession," *The Guardian*, January 8, 2020, theguardian.com/environment/2020/jan/07/honeybees-deaths-almonds-hives-aoe.

9. Ferris Jabr, "The Mind-Boggling Math of Migratory Beekeeping," *Scientific American* September 1, 2013, scientificamerican.com/article/migratory-beekeeping-mind-boggling-math/; Emily Wilder, "Bees for Hire: California Almonds Becomes Migratory Colonies Biggest Task," and *The West*, Stanford University, August, 17, 2018, andthewest.stanford.edu/2018/bees-for-hire-california-almonds-become-migratory-colonies-biggest-task.

10. Richie Nimmo, "The Bio-Politics of Bees: Industrial Farming and Colony Collapse Disorder," *Humanimalia* 6, no. 2 (2015): 1–20, doi.org/10.52537/humanimalia.9909.

11. In the context of India: Vandana Shiva, "Pesticides, GMOs, and the War Against Biodiversity," in *Queen of the Sun: What Are the Bees are Telling Us?* ed. Taggart Siegel (Sussex, UK: Clairview Books, 2012): 101-109; In the context of the United States: A.Z. Ivey-Stephenson, A.E. Crosby, S.P. Jack, T. Haileyesus, and M. Kresnow-Sedacca, "Suicide Trends Among and Within Urbanization Levels by Sex, Race/Ethnicity, Age Group, and Mechanism of Death — United States, 2001–2015," *Surveillance Summaries* 66, no. 18 (October 6, 2017): 1-16, doi.org/10.15585/mmwr.ss6618a1; Andrea Bjornestad, et al., "An Analysis of Suicide Risk Factors among Farmers in the Midwestern United States," *International Journal of Environmental Research and Public Health* 18, no. 7 (March 30, 2021): 3563, doi.org/10.3390/ijerph18073563.

12. Annette McGivney, "Like Sending Bees to War: The Truth Behind Your Almond Milk Obsession," *The Guardian*, January 8, 2020, theguardian.com/environment/2020/jan/07/honeybees-deaths-almonds-hives-aoe.

13. For more on this, consider the seminal works of Haunani-Kay Trask, such as *From a Native Daughter: Colonialism and Sovereignty in Hawaii* (Honolulu: University of Hawaii Press, 1993).

14. Keilyn Ing and Christina L. Mogren, "Evidence of Competition between Honey Bees and Hylaeus anthracinus (Hymenoptera: Colletidae), an Endangered Hawaiian Yellow-Faced Bee," *Pacific Science* 74, no. 1 (2020): 75–85, doi.org/10.2984/74.1.6; Claire Caulfield and Kevin Knodell, "Hawaii's Complicated Relationship with European Honey Bees," July 13, 2021, in *Honolulu Civil Beat*, podcast, MP3 audio, 10:13, civilbeat.org/2021/07/podcast-hawaiis-complicated-relationship-with-european-honeybees/.

THE UNDERSTORY

DEFORESTATION
On Zoonotic Disease & Global Health

1. World Health Organization, *WHO-convened global study of origins of SARS-CoV-2: China Part*, (Geneva: World Health Organization, March 2021): 92, who.int/publications/i/item/who-convened-global-study-of-origins-of-sars-cov-2-china-part.
2. World Health Organization, *WHO-convened global study of origins of SARS-CoV-2: China Part*, (Geneva: World Health Organization, March 2021): 120, who.int/publications/i/item/who-convened-global-study-of-origins-of-sars-cov-2-china-part.
3. World Health Organization, *WHO-convened global study of origins of SARS-CoV-2: China Part*, (Geneva: World Health Organization, March 2021): 7,who.int/publications/i/item/who-convened-global-study-of-origins-of-sars-cov-2-china-part.
4. Arne Ruckert, Carlos Gonçalo das Neves, John Amuasi, Suzanne Hindmarch, Christina Brux, Andrea Sylvia Winkler, and Hélène Carabin, "Policy Brief: One Health as a Pillar for a Transformative Pandemic Treaty," Global Health Centre, 2021, graduateinstitute.ch/sites/internet/files/2021-11/policybrief-onehealth-v3.pdf.
5. World Health Organization, "World Health Assembly Agrees to Launch Process to Develop Historic Global Accord on Pandemic Prevention, Preparedness and Response," December 1, 2021, who.int/news/item/01-12-2021-world-health-assembly-agrees-to-launch-process-to-develop-historic-global-accord-on-pandemic-prevention-preparedness-and-response.

6. For more, see: Obijiofor Aginam, "Beyond Covid-19: Africa and the Future of Global Health Governance," *Africa Health*, October 2021, africa-health. com/wp-content/uploads/2021/11/AH-2021-10-21-GHG.pdf; Obijiofor Aginam, "The World Health Assembly Special Session and Pandemic Treaty Controversy," Think Global Health, December 15, 2021, thinkglobalhealth. org/article/world-health-assembly-special-session-and-pandemic-treaty-controversy.

On RCMP Violence: A Note

1. Unist'ot'en Camp, "Wet'suwet'en Hereditary Chiefs Evict Coast GasLink from Territory," January 2020, unistoten.camp/ wetsuweten-hereditary-chiefs-evict-coastal-gaslink-from-territory.

REWILDING
On Silence

1. On Terminology:

> In this essay, the terms *silence, language, speaking*, and *voice* are used to portray the methods of pattern-sharing, set definition, and shared-meaning, that reside at the foundation of shared communication. This is an imperfect, somewhat ableist way to express what I mean; and at the same time, I am seeking to depict these terms beyond neurotypical, ableist frameworks that define speech as only verbal speech, listening as solely an auditory act, and silence as only the absence of physical sound. What I am curious about is both tied, and not tied, to the body.

2. On Overpopulation:

> "The consumption of the world's wealthiest 10% produces up to 50% of the planet's consumption-based CO_2 emissions, while the poorest half of humanity contributes only 10%. With a mere 26 billionaires now in possession of more wealth than half the world, this trend is likely to continue …."

> From Heather Alberro, "Why We Should Be Wary of Blaming Overpopulation for the Climate Crisis," The Conversation, January 28, 2020, theconversation.com/why-we-should-be-wary-of-blaming-overpopulation-for-the-climate-crisis-130709.

3. Ursula K. Le Guin, "Speech in acceptance of the National Book Foundation Medal" (speech, New York City, NY, November 19, 2014), ursulakleguin.com/transcript.

LAZARUS SPECIES
On the Endangered Species Act: Black-Footed Ferret v. Pipeline

1. Earl Gustky, "Black-Footed Animal, Once Believed Extinct, Has Surfaced in Wyoming; Curiosity-Seekers Head for Meeteetse: Mysterious Ferret Has 'Em Guessing," *Los Angeles Times*, March 17, 1985, latimes.com/archives/la-xpm-1985-03-17-sp-35545-story.html.
2. Holmes Rolston III, "Property Rights and Endangered Species," *University of Colorado Law Review* 61, no. 2 (1990): 283–306. mountainscholar.org/bitstream/handle/10217/37455/property-rights-U-Colo-updated.pdf.
3. Ivan Peterson, "How the (1980s) West was Won by the Black-Footed Ferret," *New York Times*, January 3, 1986, nytimes.com/1986/01/03/us/how-the-1980-s-west-was-won-by-the-black-footed-ferret.html.
4. "Black-Footed Ferrets: The Rediscovery," Wyoming Game and Fish Department, November 30, 2011, video, 2:35, youtube.com/watch?v=1U-YCXjf4_I.
5. EXP Energy Services, *Keystone XL Pipeline Project Plan of Development*, (Houston: EXP Energy Services, 2020): 130, eplanning.blm.gov/public_projects/nepa/1503435/20011515/250015757/BLM_FINAL_POD_20200117_508c.pdf.
6. Lawsuit filed by Center for Biological Diversity, Sierra Club, Montana Environmental Alliance Information Center, Friends of the Earth, and Waterkeeper Alliance, Inc., against: Lieutenant General Scott A. Spellmon, in his official capacity, and U.S. Army Corps of Engineeers, on May 3, 2021, s3-us-west-2.amazonaws.com/s3-wagtail.biolgicaldiversity.org/documents/NWP-Complaint-5-3-21.pdf.

On the Business of De-Extinction

1. Geron Corporation, *Geron and Exeter Life Sciences Merge Start Licensing and ViaGen to Form Combined Licensing and Operating Company for Animal Cloning Technologies*, (Foster City: Geron Corporation, 2008), docoh.com/filing/886744/0001157523-08-006775/GERN-8K; Precigen Incorporated, *Annual Report: Form 10-K Trexon Corp* (Washington, D.C.: Security and Exchange Commission, March 2, 2020), sec.report/Document/0001628280-20-002699/; "Advancing Medicine with Precision," Precigen, precigen.com.
2. Jessica Baron, "If You Love Animals, Don't Clone Your Pet," *Forbes*, December 24, 2018, forbes.com/sites/jessicabaron/2018/12/24/if-you-love-animals-dont-clone-your-pet.

3. Hwang Woo-suk et al., "Patient-Specific Embryonic Stem Cells Derived from Human SCNT Blastocysts," *Science* 308, no. 5729 (June 17, 2005): 1777-83, doi.org/10.1126/science.1112286; D. Cyranoski, "Woo Suk Hwang Convicted, But Not of Fraud," *Nature* 461, no. 1181 (2009), doi.org/10.1038/461181a.

4. "Revive & Restore Staff," Revive & Restore, reviverestore.org/about-us; Bill Berkrot, "Medco Buys Genetic Services Company DNA Direct," Reuters, February 2, 2010, reuters.com/article/ us-medco-dna-idUSTRE6110VE20100202.

MOUNTAIN THAT EATS MEN
On the Lithium Coup

1. For more on this, see: Kathleen Schroeder, "Economic Globalization and Bolivia's Regional Divide," *Journal of Latin American Geography* 6, no. 2 (2007): 99–120, doi.org/10.1353/lag.2007.0048; Brooke Larson, Raúl Madrid, René Antonio Mayorga, and Jessica Varat, "Bolivia: Social Movements, Populism, and Democracy," Woodrow Wilson Center, August 2008, wilsoncenter.org/publication/bolivia-social-movements-populism-and-democracy.

2. Edward C. Keefer, Douglas Kraft, and James Seikmeier, eds. "Document 76a. Editorial Note." *Foreign Relations of the United States, 1969–1976, Volume E–10, Documents on American Republics, 1969–1972,* (Washington, D.C.: Office of the Historian, Bureau of Public Affairs, 2009), history.state.gov/ historicaldocuments/frus1969-76ve10/d76a.

3. Jake Johnston and David Rosnick, "Observing the Observers: The OAS in the 2019 Bolivian Elections," Centre for Economic Policy Research, March 2020, cepr.net/wp-content/uploads/2020/03/bolivia-2020-3.pdf.

4. Jake Johnston, "Data from Bolivia's Election add more evidence that OAS Fabricated Last Year's Fraud Claims," Centre for Economic Policy Research, October 21, 2020, cepr.net/data-from-bolivias-election-add-more-evidence-that-oas-fabricated-last-years-fraud-claims.

BLOOD STONES: AN INVENTORY
On Diamonds

1. Nathan Munier, *The Political Economy of the Kimberley Process* (Cambridge: Cambridge University Press 2020), 62.

2. This data was reported as part of a seminal report by Global Witness that led to international regulation of the diamond trade and the Kimberley Process: Global Witness, "A Rough Trade: The Role of Companies and Government in the Angolan Conflict," December 1, 1998, cdn2.globalwitness.org/archive/ files/pdfs/a_rough_trade.pdf.

3. On Conflict Diamonds in Angola, as reported by the *Washington Post*:

> "In the 1990s, when an explosion of diamonds from Angola burst onto the world market and threatened a glut that would reduce prices, De Beers mopped up those diamonds. Those Angolan diamonds were from the illicit mines of the UNITA rebel movement, which had seized rich diamond territories and quickly began making billions—to buy arms and continue a war that has raged for 25 years.... Explaining why his company bought a product it now condemns, Lamont said in e-mail, 'Up until this date [1998], there was no international law/resolution in place prohibiting the trade of any commodity other than arms from Angola.'"

From Lynne Duke, "Diamond Trade's Tragic Flaw," *Washington Post*, April 29, 2001, washingtonpost.com/archive/business/2001/04/29/diamond-trades-tragic-flaw/b4c2c3c4-f5a8-4ba7-9d96-c9a8f80945a1.

4. Cecilia Gardner, "Industry Braces for Blowback from 'Blood Diamond,'" interview by Frank Langfitt, October 20, 2006, in *All Things Considered*, produced by NPR, radio, MP3, audio, 4:55, npr.org/2006/10/20/6353402/industry-braces-for-blowback-from-blood-diamond.

5. On the Kimberley Process, as stated by the organization:

> "The Kimberley Process is an international certification scheme that regulates trade in rough diamonds. It aims to prevent the flow of conflict diamonds, while helping to protect legitimate trade in rough diamonds. The Kimberley Process Certification Scheme (KPCS) outlines the rules that govern the trade in rough diamonds. The KPCS has developed a set of minimum requirements that each participant must meet. The KP is not, strictly speaking, an international organization: it has no permanent offices or permanent staff. It relies on the contributions—under the principle of "burden-sharing"—of participants, supported by industry and civil society observers. Neither can the KP be considered as an international agreement from a legal perspective, as it is implemented through the national legislations of its participants."

From "What is the Kimberley Process?" Kimberley Process, kimberleyprocess.com/en/what-kp.

6. Global Witness, "Global Witness leaves Kimberley Process, Calls for Diamond Trade to be Held Accountable," December 2, 2011, globalwitness.org/en/archive/global-witness-leaves-kimberley-process-calls-diamond-trade-be-held-accountable. For more on this, see: Global Witness, "Why We Are Leaving the Kimberley Process," December 2, 2011, globalwitness.org/en/archive/why-we-are-leaving-kimberley-process-message-global-witness-founding-director-charmian-gooch.

7. Attawapiskat First Nation, "Attawapiskat First Nation versus De Beers Diamond Mine," The Bullet, October 2, 2020, socialistproject.ca/2020/10/attawapiskat-first-nation-vs-debeers-diamond-mine; Rita Celli, "How CBC Found the Secret Diamond Royalty," CBC News, May 12, 2015, cbc.ca/news/business/how-cbc-found-the-secret-diamond-royalty-1.3065765; "Victor Mine," De Beers, canada.debeersgroup.com/operations/mining/victor-mine.

8. John Ahni Schertow, "Attawapiskat Holding Winter Blockade against De Beers," Intercontinental Cry, February 25, 2009, intercontinentalcry.org/attawapiskat-holding-winter-blockade-against-de-beers.

9. CBC News, "De Beers Pleads Guilty to Failing to Report Mercury Monitoring Data Near Northern Ontario Mine," July 6, 2021, cbc.ca/news/canada/sudbury/debeers-court-timmins-mercury-pollution-case-1.6091664.

10. Brett Forester, "Attawapiskat Fighting De Beers Bid to Build 3rd Landfill at Closed Mine," APTN News, September 30, 2020, aptnnews.ca/national-news/attawapiskat-fighting-de-beers-bid-to-build-3rd-landfill-at-closed-mine/.

11. Attawapiskat First Nation, "DeBeers Victor Diamond Mine Pushing for Massive Garbage Dump in Fragile Wetlands Habitat—Attawapiskat First Nation Fighting Back," Newswire, September 28, 2020, newswire.ca/news-releases/debeers-victor-diamond-mine-pushing-for-massive-garbage-dump-in-fragile-wetlands-habitat-attawapiskat-first-nation-fighting-back-877062006.html.

THE ROMANCE OF FLOODS
On Structural Violence

1. René Lemarchand, "Review of 'Development Agencies and Structural Violence in Rwanda,' by Peter Uvin," *International Studies Review* 1, no. 3 (1999): 160–64, jstor.org/stable/3186343; Paul Farmer, "On Suffering and Structural Violence: A View from Below," *Race/Ethnicity: Multidisciplinary Global Contexts* 3, no. 1 (2009): 11–28, jstor.org/stable/25595022; Tamar Diana Wilson and Annelou Ypeij, "Tourism, Gender, and Ethnicity," *Latin American Perspectives* 39, no. 6 (November 2012): 5–16, doi.org/10.1177/0094582X12453896.

2. Peter Uvin, "Development Aid and Structural Violence: The Case of Rwanda," *Development* 42, no. 3 (1999): 49–56, doi.org/10.1057/palgrave.development.1110060.

3. On the Gini-Index in Brazil:

    "In 2021, Brazil's level of wealth inequality stood at ninth in the world, as measured by the World Bank."

    From The World Bank, "Gini-Index - Brazil," data.worldbank.org/indicator/SI.POV.GINI?end=2019&locations=BR.

RARE HONEY
On Survival

1. Jen St. Denis, "Meet the Indigenous-Led Organizations Saving Lives in the Downtown Eastside," The Tyee, September 1, 2021, thetyee.ca/News/2021/09/01/Indigenous-Led-Organizations-Saving-Lives-DTES.

2. Gabor Maté (@gabormatemd), "Addiction is not a choice anyone makes …" Instagram photo, August 12, 2021, instagram.com/p/CSe7da_LYv1/.

3. "Vancouver's Approach to the Overdose Crisis," City of Vancouver, vancouver.ca/people-programs/drugs.aspx.; "The Incite Story," PHS Community Services Society, July 28, 2020, phs.ca/the-insite-story.

SELECTED
BIBLIOGRAPHY

IN ADDITION TO the sources cited in the end notes, these works were referenced within the essays, and/or provided insight, information, and food for thought.

INTRODUCTION

Barry, Andrew, and Mark Maslin. "The politics of the anthropocene: a dialogue." *Geo: Geography and Environment* 3, no. 2 (September 26, 2016). doi.org/10.1002/geo2.22.

Büscher, Bram, and Robert Fletcher. "The Word 'Anthropocene' is Failing Us: Bram Büscher and Robert Fletcher Propose Some Alternatives." Literary Hub, February 14, 2020. lithub.com/the-word-anthropocene-is-failing-us.

Erickson, Bruce. "Anthropocene Futures: Linking Colonialism and Environmentalism in an Age of Crisis." *Environment and Planning D: Society and Space* 38, no. 1 (February 2020): 111–28. doi.org/10.1177/0263775818806514.

Hanh, Thich Nhat. *The Art of Living*. New York: HarperCollins, 2017, quoted in Thich Nhat Hanh, Garrison Institute, "The Insight of Interbeing." garrisoninstitute.org/blog/insight-of-interbeing.

Haraway, Donna. "Anthropocene, Capitalocene, Plantationocene, Chthulucene: Making Kin." *Environmental Humanities* 6, no. 1 (May 1, 2015), 159–165. doi.org/10.1215/22011919-3615934.

McKie, Robin. "How our colonial past altered the ecobalance of an entire planet," *The Guardian*, June 10, 2018. theguardian.com/science/2018/jun/10/colonialism-changed-earth-geology-claim-scientists.

Moore, Jason W., ed. *Anthropocene or Capitalocene?: Nature, History, and the Crisis of Capitalism*. Oakland, CA: PM Press, 2016.

Vaughan-Lee, Emmanuel. "Speaking the Anthropocene: An Interview with Robert Macfarlane," *Emergence Magazine*, May 30, 2019. Recorded interview, 76 min. emergencemagazine.org/interview/speaking-the-anthropocene/.

Yusoff, Kathryn. "Anthropogenesis: Origins and Endings in the Anthropocene." *Theory, Culture & Society* 33, no. 2 (March 2016): 3–28. doi.org/10.1177/0263276415581021.

Yusoff, Kathryn. *A Billion Black Anthropocenes or None*. Minneapolis: University of Minnesota Press, 2018.

Zalasiewicz, Jan, Mark Williams, Alan Smith, Tiffany L. Barry, Angela L. Coe, Paul R. Bown, Patrick Brenchley, et al. "Are we now living in the Anthropocene?" *GSA Today* 18, no. 2 (February 2008): 4–8. doi.org/10.1130/GSAT01802A.1.

DEFORESTATION

Bouchard, C., et al. "Increased risk of tick-borne diseases with climate and environmental changes." *Canada Communicable Disease Report* 45, no. 4 (April 4, 2019): 81–89. doi.org/10.14745/ccdr.v45i04a02.

Everard, Mark, Paul Johnston, David Santillo, Chad Staddon. "The role of ecosystems in mitigation and management of Covid-19 and other zoonoses." *Environmental Science & Policy* 111, (September 2020): 7–17. doi.org/10.1016/j.envsci.2020.05.017.

Lawler, Odette K., et al. "The COVID-19 Pandemic Is Intricately Linked to Biodiversity Loss and Ecosystem Health." *The Lancet. Planetary Health* 5, no. 11 (November 2021): e840–e850. doi.org/10.1016/S2542-5196(21)00258-8.

Saker, L., K. Lee, B. Cannito, A. Gilmore A, D. Campbell-Lendrum. *Globalization and infectious diseases: A review of the linkages*. Switzerland: World Health Organization on behalf of the Special Programme for Research and Training in Tropical Diseases, 2004. apps.who.int/iris/bitstream/handle/10665/68726/TDR_STR_SEB_ST_04.2.pdf.

REWILDING

Dillard, Annie. *Teaching a Stone to Talk: Expeditions and Encounters*. New York: Harper and Row, 1982.

Monbiot, George. "For More Wonder, Rewild the World." TedX. September 2013. Video, 14:57. ted.com/talks/george_monbiot_for_more_wonder_rewild_the_world, quoted in "How Wolves Change Rivers." Sustainable Human. February 4, 2022. Video, 4:11. youtu.be/W88Sact1kws.

LAZARUS SPECIES

Allen, Jessica, David M. Doyle, Shane McCorristine, Aisling McMahon. "De-Extinction, Regulation and Nature Conservation." *Journal of Environmental Law* 32, no. 2 (July 2020): 309–322. doi.org/10.1093/jel/eqaa009.

Barnhill-Dilling, K., and J. Delborne. "Whose intentions? What consequences? Interrogating 'Intended Consequences' for conservation with environmental biotechnology." *Conservation Science and Practice* 3, no. 4 (April 6, 2021). doi.org/10.1111/csp2.406.

Biggins, Dean E., and Max H. Schroeder. "Historical and Present Status of the Black-Footed Ferret." Great Plains Wildlife Damage Control Workshop Proceedings, 1987. digitalcommons.unl.edu/gpwdcwp/50/.

Brister, E., and A. Newhouse. "Not the Same Old Chestnut: Rewilding Forests with Biotechnology." *Environmental Ethics* 42, no. 2 (Summer 2020): 149–167. doi.org/10.5840/enviroethics2020111614.

Burgiel, Stanley W., et al. "Exploring the intersections of governance, constituencies, and risk in genetic interventions." *Conservation Science and Practice* 3, no. 4 (April 2021). doi.org/10.1111/csp2.380.

Davidson, Ana, Elizabeth Hunter, Jon Erz, David Lightfoot, Aliya McCarthy, Jennifer Mueller, and Kevin Shoemaker. "Reintroducing a keystone burrowing rodent to restore an arid North American grassland: challenges and successes" *Restoration Ecology* 26, no. 5 (September 2018): 909-920. doi.org/10.1111/rec.12671.

Duncan, David E. "Inside the Very Big, Very Controversial Business of Dog Cloning," *Vanity Fair*, August 7, 2018. vanityfair.com/style/2018/08/dog-cloning-animal-sooam-hwang.

Novak, B.J., T. Maloney, and R. Phelan. "Advancing a New Toolkit for Conservation: From Science to Policy." *The CRISPR Journal* 1, no. 1 (2018): 11–15. doi.org/10.1089/crispr.2017.0019.

Novak, B.J., R. Phelan, and M. Weber. "U.S. conservation translocations: Over a century of intended consequences." *Conservation Science and Practice* 3, no. 4 (April 2021). doi.org/10.1111/csp2.394.

Phelan, R, Bridget Baumgartner, Stewart Brand, Evelyn Brister, Stanley W. Burgiel, et al. "Intended Consequences Statement." *Conservation Science and Practice* 3, no. 4 (April 2021): e371. doi.org/10.1111/csp2.371.

Preston, C. *The Synthetic Age: Outdesigning Evolution, Resurrecting Species, and Reengineering Our World*. Cambridge, MA: MIT Press, 2018.

Ryder, O.A., C. Friese, H.T. Greely, et al. "Exploring the limits of saving a subspecies: The ethics and social dynamics of restoring northern white rhinos (*Ceratotherium simum cottoni*)." *Conservation Science and Practice* 2, no. 8 (August 2020): e241. doi.org/10.1111/csp2.241.

Smith, Douglas W. and Rolf O. Peterson. "Intended and unintended consequences of wolf restoration to Yellowstone and Isle Royale National Parks." *Conservation Science and Practice* 3, no. 4 (April 2021): e413. doi.org/10.1111/csp2.413.

THE PLASTER CITIZENS OF POMPEII

Acocella, Joan. "The Terror and the Fascination of Pompeii." *The New Yorker*, February 10, 2020. newyorker.com/magazine/2020/02/17/the-terror-and-the-fascination-of-pompeii.

"AD 79: Eyewitness Account of the Eruption of Mount Vesuvius." *Bulletin of the Art Institute of Chicago (1973–1982)* 72, no. 4 (1978): 4–7. doi.org/10.2307/4104138.

Elliot, Josh K. "Canadian 'cursed' by stolen Pompeii relics returns them with a 'sorry.'" Global News, October 14, 2020. globalnews.ca/news/7396332/pompeii-curse-bad-luck-artifacts-canadian.

Stewart, Lain S., and Luigi Piccardi. "Seismic faults and sacred sanctuaries in Aegean antiquity." *Proceedings of the Geologists' Association* 128, no. 5–6 (2017): 711–721. doi.org/10.1016/j.pgeola.2017.07.009.

MOUNTAIN THAT EATS MEN

Anandakugan, Nithyani. "Hopes for a Rainy Day: A History of Bolivia's Water Crisis." *Harvard International Review*, July 2, 2020. hir.harvard.edu/hopes-for-a-rainy-day-a-history-of.

Assies, Willem. "David versus Goliath in Cochabamba: Water Rights, Neoliberalism, and the Revival of Social Protest in Bolivia." *Latin American Perspectives* 30, no. 3 (2003): 14–36. jstor.org/stable/3185034.

"Bechtel Perspective on the Aguas del Tunari Water Concession in Cochabamba, Bolivia." Bechtel, December 2005. bechtel.com/files/perspective-aguas-del-tunari-water-concession.

"Bolivia's Rich Mountain Continues to Give." *Bloomberg News*. August 13, 2020. bnnbloomberg.ca/bolivia-s-rich-mountain-continues-to-give-1.1479050.

Calzadilla, Paola Villavicencio, and Louis J. Kotzé. "Living in Harmony with Nature? A Critical Appraisal of the Rights of Mother Earth in Bolivia." *Transnational Environmental Law* 7, no. 3 (2018): 397–424. doi.org/10.1017/S2047102518000201.

Crowther, Herbert. "Bolivia's Role in the Energy Transition Threatened by Lithium Uncertainty." The Atlantic Council. August 6, 2018. atlanticcouncil.org/commentary/energysource-explains-bolivia-s-role-in-energy-transition-threatened-by-lithium-uncertainty.

Galeano, Eduardo. *Open Veins of Latin America: Five Centuries of the Pillage of a Continent* New York: Monthly Review Press, 1973.

Smith, Adam. *An Inquiry into the Nature and Causes of the Wealth of Nations.* London, UK: Oxford University Press, 2008. First published in 1776 by W. Strahan and T. Cadell, London.

World Heritage Centre/ICOMOS. "Reactive Monitoring Mission to the City of Potosí, Plurinational State of Bolivia." UNESCO. January 30, 2014. whc.unesco.org/en/documents/128573.

Westoll, Andrew. "The Mountain That Eats Men." *The Walrus*, January/February 2009. thewalrus.ca/2009-01-travel.

BLOOD STONES: AN INVENTORY

"A Games of Stones." Global Witnesss. June 2017. globalwitness.org/en/campaigns/central-african-republic-car/game-of-stones.

Hummel, Joseph. "Diamonds Are a Smuggler's Best Friend: Regulation, Economics, and Enforcement in the Global Effort to Curb the Trade in Conflict Diamonds." *The International Lawyer* 41, no. 4 (2007): 1145–1169. jstor.org/stable/40707834.

Kirkup, James. "Beautiful Gems Help Alliance Pay for 5-Year War." *Seattle Times.* November 21, 2001. archive.seattletimes.com/archive/ ?date=20011121&slug=jewels21&fbclid=I.

Obale, Offah. "From Conflict to Illicit: Mapping the Diamond Trade from Central African Republic to Cameroon." Partnership Africa Canada. December 2016. impacttransform.org/wp-content/uploads/2017/09/2016-Dec-From-Conflict-to-Illicit-Mapping-the-diamond-trade-from-Central-African-Republic-to-Cameroon.pdf.

Pallister, David, and Chris McGreal. "De Beers: Diamonds No Longer a Guerrilla's Best Friend." *The Guardian.* March 27, 2000. theguardian.com/world/2000/mar/28/davidpallister.chrismcgreal.

"Pompeii Archeologists Uncover 'Sorcerer's Treasure Trove.'" *BBC News.* August 12, 2019. bbc.com/news/world-europe-49325627.

Winetroub, Andrew H. "A Diamond Scheme Is Forever Lost: The Kimberley Process's Deteriorating Tripartite Structure and Its Consequences for the Scheme's Survival." *Indiana Journal of Global Legal Studies* 20, no. 2 (2013): 1425–44. doi.org/10.2979/indjglolegstu.20.2.1425.

Zwick, Edward, dir. *Blood Diamond*. Los Angeles: Warner Bothers, 2006.

A BRIEF HISTORY OF MERMAIDS

Andersen, Hans Christian. *The Little Mermaid*, trans. M.R. James. London: Faber & Faber, 1953. First published in 1837 by C.A. Reitzel, Copenhagen.

Gerstein, Mordicai. *The Seal Mother.* New York: Dial Books, 1986.

Howard, Ron, dir. *Splash.* Los Angeles: Buena Vista Pictures, 1984.

FLOCK MEMORY

Maté, Gabor. *In the Realm of Hungry Ghosts: Close Encounters with Addiction.* Toronto: Knopf Canada, 2008.

THE FAILSAFE

Bee Dancer. "Bee Queen." YouTube. January 30, 2012. Video, 12:09. youtu.be/iTLgSqu4r3E.

Marquez, Gabriel García. *Love in the Time of Cholera.* London, UK: Penguin Classics, 2016. First English edition published in 1988 by Alfred A. Knopf, New York.

Nelson, Peter. *The Pollinators.* Accord, NY: Stonykill Films, 2020.

ABOUT THE AUTHOR

ALESSANDRA NACCARATO is a writer and poet born and raised in Tkaronto (Toronto). The recipient of the 2015 RBC Bronwen Wallace Award for Emerging Writers and the 2017 CBC Poetry Prize, her poetry and essays have appeared widely in publications such as *The New Quarterly, Room Magazine,* and *Event.* She holds an MFA in Creative Writing from the University of British Columbia, and a graduate degree in Community Economic Development from Concordia University, supporting two decades of work and research in grassroots social change, community arts, and the prevention of gender-based violence. Her debut poetry collection, *Re-Origin of Species,* was awarded the AICW Bressani Literary Prize for Poetry, shortlisted for the Gerald Lampert Memorial Award, longlisted for the Pat Lowther Memorial Award, and named a Best Book of 2019 by CBC Books.

ABOUT THE
ESSAIS SERIES

DRAWING ON THE Old and Middle French definitions of *essai*, meaning first "trial" and then "attempt," and from which the English word "essay" emerges, the works in the Essais Series challenge traditional forms and styles of cultural enquiry. The Essais Series is committed to publishing works concerned with justice, equity, and diversity. It supports texts that draw on seemingly intractable questions, to ask them anew and to elaborate these questions. The books in the Essais Series are forms of vital generosity; they invite attention to a necessary reconsideration of culture, society, politics, and experience.

For more information visit bookhugpress.ca/product-category/essais-series/.

COLOPHON

Manufactured as the first edition of
Imminent Domains: Reckoning with the Anthropocene
in the fall of 2022 by Book*hug Press

Edited for the press by Linda Pruessen
Copy edited by Shannon Whibbs
Additional editorial assistance by Charlene Chow
Proofread by Hazel Millar, Jay Millar, and Charlene Chow
Typeset by Lind Design
Type: Arno Pro and Sackers Gothic

Printed in Canada

bookhugpress.ca